AMERICAN SIGN LANGUAGE MADE EASY FOR BEGINNERS

A VISUAL GUIDE WITH ASL SIGNS, LESSONS, AND QUIZZES

TRAVIS BELMONTES-MERRELL

PHOTOGRAPHY BY JAMES BUETI

callisto
publishing
an imprint of Sourcebooks

To my daughter, Emilia Rose. I love you more than words can say. You have my heart forever.

Published by Callisto Publishing LLC C/O Sourcebooks LLC
P.O. Box 4410, Naperville, Illinois 60567-4410
(630) 961-3900
callistopublishing.com

Printed and Bound In China
OGP 11

CONTENTS

INTRODUCTION vi

CHAPTER 1: LEARNING ASL 1

CHAPTER 2: THE BASICS: ABCs, 123s & BEYOND 17

CHAPTER 3: GREETINGS & PEOPLE 27

CHAPTER 4: THOUGHTS & FEELINGS 53

CHAPTER 5: DAILY ROUTINES 79

CHAPTER 6: TIME & PLACE 101

CHAPTER 7: FOOD & DRINK 129

CHAPTER 8: ACTIVITIES & EVENTS 157

CHAPTER 9: TRAVEL 183

CHAPTER 10: HEALTH, SAFETY & COLORS 211

ANSWER KEY 243

RESOURCES 258

REFERENCES 260

INDEX 261

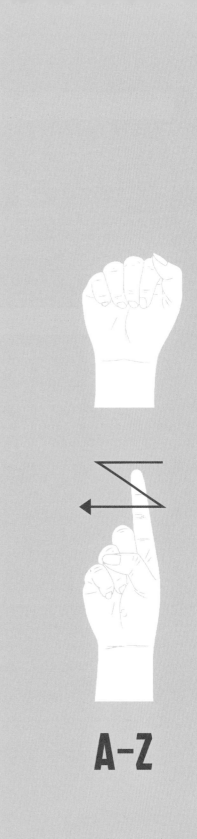

A–Z

INTRODUCTION

Welcome to *American Sign Language Made Easy for Beginners*. I'm glad you've decided to take the first step to learn American Sign Language (ASL). Learning a language is never an easy journey; however, it can be fun and rewarding, and this book will provide you with a variety of resources to help you along your way.

My own journey with learning ASL has involved many milestones. At the age of three, I was diagnosed with meningitis, from which I became hard of hearing. I grew up as the only Deaf member of my family; however, my parents could see early on that I had a strong interest in learning ASL. Although I did not formally learn ASL until high school, my parents made sure I understood my identity as a Deaf person and encouraged me to challenge myself in everything I did. When I learned my high school offered ASL as a foreign language, I knew this was going to be the beginning of a new chapter in my life. I remember walking into my first day of class and getting my first ASL textbook. I flipped the pages, eager to begin. Right then, I said to myself, *One day, I want to be an author of an ASL textbook to help teach others American Sign Language*.

Throughout high school, my family and teachers were supportive of my passion to learn ASL. I was inspired by my teacher, who provided me with the skills to be a lifelong learner and the drive to further my education in ASL. At community college, I deepened my knowledge about Deaf culture and was welcomed into the Deaf community with open arms.

I took a pause from learning ASL when I met my husband, moved to a new city, and attended a university where ASL was not offered. I graduated with a bachelor's degree in journalism and worked at a TV news station. Still, I felt like something was missing. I returned to school and earned my teaching certification. While teaching general education, I decided to attend a nearby community college to continue learning ASL. Shortly after, I gained my credentials to teach ASL in 2017.

I thoroughly enjoyed teaching ASL and seeing the interactions my students received when they attended Deaf events. I wanted to expand my knowledge of the language and culture and learn how to teach it more effectively. I returned once again to school, where my professors and classmates gave me the strong foundation I needed to be a successful student and a valued member of the Deaf community. I graduated with my master's degree in teaching ASL in 2018.

I am currently the program coordinator at the University of Texas at Arlington. ASL will always be part of my life; I intend to share all my knowledge and passion with everyone I meet. And I'm finally able to share that book I promised I would write.

American Sign Language Made Easy for Beginners will provide you with the foundation to understand the sentence structure and grammar of ASL. The book also contains 400-plus vocabulary words and instructions for signing them. There is much more to learn than could ever be contained in these pages, but it is my hope that this book will open the door for you, too, to become a lifelong learner of ASL.

CHAPTER 1

LEARNING ASL

In this chapter, you'll learn a brief history of ASL, the building blocks of signing, and an overview of how the lessons and vocabulary that follow can help you apply and master your new skills. Let's dive in.

HOW TO USE THIS BOOK

American Sign Language Made Easy for Beginners is designed for true beginners. Although this book is self-guided, its intent is to give you the feeling of learning the language where you are, without having to be in the classroom with an instructor. The themes and vocabulary for each chapter have been carefully selected and organized to maximize your learning of the language for optimum usefulness. Lessons provided at the end of each chapter will help you polish your signing skills and learn about Deaf communities and cultures.

This book begins with the building blocks of American Sign Language (ASL), including the alphabet, fingerspelling, and numbers. As you progress through the chapters, you'll build on vocabulary from previous chapters. Once you complete a new chapter and lessons, it can be helpful to refer back to previous chapters periodically to refresh your memory on vocabulary and additional information.

Cultural discussions, grammar, and syntax will be presented throughout the book. Although we cannot cover every Deaf culture fact, grammar rule, and syntax style that exists in the wide world of ASL, we'll provide the basics you need to get started. Nothing beats real-world exposure, so the more you can immerse yourself in your local Deaf community, the better you'll be able to expand your knowledge.

This book is designed to introduce topics and words in a particular order in which it's recommended you study, but feel free to move around the chapters in whatever way fits your learning style.

GO AT YOUR OWN PACE

Just like other languages, ASL is not a language that you can learn in a few days, weeks, or even months. Learning a language takes time, sometimes years, to fully master; but the fun part is that you can start using ASL as soon as you learn your first sign. The lessons aren't time-bound, so go at whatever pace feels right. If you're not ready to practice phrases or sentences, or aren't ready for grammar lessons, go ahead and skip that section and dive further into vocabulary, then go back later. This book can be as flexible as you want it to be.

A few tips on how you can improve your signing skills:

Practice. Anything is done better and learned more quickly with practice. You don't have to carve out special time. Feel free to practice a sign while you're waiting in line or drinking your morning coffee.

Sign in front of a mirror, or video-record yourself. Doing this allows you to watch yourself signing and check for correct production of the signs.

Join Deaf groups or organizations with Deaf people. This is a great way to apply your knowledge from this book.

One more note: Don't get discouraged if you don't sign "perfectly" when you communicate with a Deaf person. They will surely appreciate your efforts and might offer you guidance. Take advantage of this opportunity to improve your signing and communicate more effectively—learning a new language opens doors!

LEARNING ASL, SIMPLIFIED

ASL is a language used by Deaf people and members within the Deaf community in the United States and many parts of Canada. Through the years, ASL has become one of the most widely learned languages and is now taught in K–12 schools, colleges, and universities, as well as on various social media platforms. Many different forms of sign language exist around the world, and they vary greatly in grammar structure and vocabulary. Within the United States alone, there are multiple forms of sign language, including Black American Sign Language (BASL), Pidgin Signed English (PSE), and Signing Exact English (SEE). In this book, we'll be focusing only on American Sign Language.

American Sign Language Made Easy for Beginners is designed as a guide for beginners to learn ASL simply and at one's own pace, one sign at a time. The book uses a variety of approaches to ensure optimum comprehension. Like with any language, mastering ASL requires practice, so the lessons in this book will focus on new words, while also reintroducing words from previous chapters in order to cement that knowledge. Each vocabulary word you'll learn includes both a photo and an easy-to-follow written description of how it's performed. And as you progress, we'll raise the bar with a few more challenges.

Next, we'll explore the various learning approaches used to teach the lessons in the later chapters.

STRATEGIES

I'll say it again: practice. It's one of the most essential components to grasping any new language. To help facilitate this, the lessons here are organized into themes for real-life utility, as opposed to a listing of seemingly random vocabulary words. You'll focus on word frequency rather than fluency, to quickly be able to understand and communicate individual words. The more times you see a word and practice it, the more skilled you'll become in using it.

Another piece of advice that will help you along your journey: Always use your dominant hand when signing. Using the dominant hand as the focal point and the nondominant hand as the "supporting" hand will help ensure comprehension. For example, if you're right-handed, you'll want to use your right hand for the signs and fingerspelling, and only use your left hand to help the dominant hand as needed for supporting the sign.

The vocabulary words presented in this book are illustrated with the English words printed next to the picture. This is a common strategy for learning and reading signs in a book. When reading and analyzing the vocabulary signs, always sign from the signer's perspective—that is, exactly as they are presented in the pictures. Words signed from the receiver's perspective would appear backward. Therefore, for best practices when signing with a Deaf person, it's best to be facing them.

Finally, it's important to note that in ASL, some signs have regional variations. If you're unsure of which sign to use, ask a member of the local Deaf community.

LESSONS

The design and structure of every chapter within this book are created with you, the learner, in mind. At the end of each chapter, lessons with exercises will give you the opportunity to practice signs and phrases, as well as the proper structure of ASL messages. This book is designed to support different learning styles—visual and tactile—that's why you'll see both pictures and texts presented within the lessons. All the sentences and word exercises reflect real-life communication scenarios, designed to strengthen your expressive skills and help prepare you for real-world experiences.

Throughout this book, you'll also find tips and strategies that will help increase your knowledge of ASL and its culture. Tips provide extra support and learning tools for remembering the vocabulary, such as using a visual example to help you recall and understand signs, concepts, or phrases. Some tips come in the form of a cultural discussion, to better explain why the Deaf community uses a particular concept or phrase.

GRAMMAR AND SYNTAX

Since English sentence structure is different from the structure of ASL, English translations are provided for ASL sentences. These will clarify the meanings of the sentences and help you begin to understand the differences in structure.

Some words in the English language don't have a corresponding sign. Examples include "and," "is," "the," "of," and "or." These words are expressed through other methods, such as facial expressions, pointing, and role-shifting; you'll learn about these concepts later in the book in the specific vocabulary word descriptions.

A BRIEF HISTORY OF AMERICAN SIGN LANGUAGE

Signed languages have been around as long as language has existed; however, sign language was not officially established as a language until 1817.

In 1815, hearing minister Thomas Hopkins Gallaudet traveled to Europe to study methods to help educate Deaf people. While studying in England, Gallaudet met educators Abbé Roch-Ambroise Cucurron Sicard and Jean Massieu, who invited him to visit their school in Paris. While in Paris, Gallaudet met Laurent Clerc, a teacher of the Deaf who was also Deaf himself, and convinced Clerc to travel back to America to help teach Deaf students. On their journey back to America, Gallaudet taught Clerc English, and Clerc taught Gallaudet sign language. Together, they would go on to create what is now known as ASL.

In 1817, the two men established the first Deaf school in Hartford, Connecticut, called The Connecticut Asylum for the Education and Instruction of Deaf and Dumb Persons (historically, the word "dumb" referred to a person who may have been mute or had the inability to speak; the school still operates today, and is now called the American School for the Deaf). This made Laurent Clerc the first official Deaf teacher of Deaf students in America.

ASL was not recognized as an official language for Deaf people until 1965, when William Stokoe, a historical linguist, published a book that identified ASL as being a true language with its own structure and grammar. As an English teacher at Gallaudet University, Stokoe spent time observing ASL and the students on campus communicating with one another. He began researching and publishing works on the language and proposed a theory to say that ASL was a true language with its own grammar and structure. Although his theory was unpopular with some, his proposition transformed ASL and its history forever. Since then, the number of people learning ASL has continued to grow considerably in the United States and Canada—according to a 2019 *Newsweek* article, about one million people were using ASL as their main form of communication.

THE WIDE WORLD OF ASL

There is a vast, diverse world of Deaf and hard of hearing people and communities speaking ASL. This book isn't meant to replace or replicate that deeper ASL education, but rather to serve as a supplemental guide and resource for learning at home. To master learning ASL, or any language, immersing oneself in the community is key. As you hone your skills, it's also important to develop a deeper understanding of Deaf culture.

In the Resources section (page 258), you will find a list of valuable and verified websites and tools that can help expand your knowledge of ASL. Another excellent way to learn and develop your signing skills is by taking an ASL course at a community college or university, or even at your local library.

DIALECTS

When it comes to dialect, or regional variations of a language, ASL is no different from spoken languages. Much like spoken languages have distinct accents, vocabulary, grammar, and pronunciation throughout different parts of a country, such regional variations can also be found in ASL. Instead of relying on spoken words, ASL accents involve a variety of signs and regional differences in how they're presented.

How do you know what a regional difference is as opposed to a completely different sign? In short, regional differences may vary by one or more of five parameters of ASL (handshape, location, movement, palm orientation, and nonmanual markers/facial expressions). An example of a regional difference would be the sign for Halloween. People use variations for signing this word. The sign can be altered by handshape, using either an H handshape or an open C handshape going over the eye region or the whole face like a mask.

Regional differences can be seen in ASL signs, but not all signs will have regional differences in every state. Signs in ASL are developed and passed on through Deaf schools, Deaf families, and communities, and they often vary from place to place. It's important to be aware of regional differences, as there may be signs that may have multiple meanings in different regions of the United States.

OTHER SIGN LANGUAGES

As its name might imply, ASL is not a universal language. ASL is primarily used in the United States and parts of Canada. Different countries have their own versions of sign language, similar to spoken languages. Even within countries, it's common to have more than one sign language used in a Deaf community. For example, sign languages with varying grammar structures in the United States include ASL; Signing Exact English (SEE); and Pidgin Signed English (PSE), or Signed English (SE). Each form of sign language is used by various Deaf community members. Pidgin Signed English/Signed English (PSE/SE) is a common mode of communication used by Deaf community members in the United States and Canada. PSE/SE structure follows the English word order, using most, if not all, of the words in the English translation. Signing Exact English (SEE) uses signs or fingerspelling for every word in the English sentence in the exact English word order. The Deaf person's learning experience—whether that involves public or private school, a hearing family or Deaf family, and/or a Deaf institute—will influence which method of sign language they use.

A LIVING LANGUAGE

ASL is a living and ever-changing language. Similar to other languages, terms and translations constantly evolve. As language develops and changes over time, ASL signs also change and adapt to modern influences. As you study more deeply, it's important to know that some signs from older books may be outdated and not used as often. In this book, you will see the most up-to-date versions of signs currently being used in the Deaf communities in the United States and Canada.

As some signs change and adapt to modern-day influences, others maintain the same translation as their original intent, even if the sign itself is no longer universally appropriate. An example of these are gendered signs. The sign for "girl," for example, is often compared to tying a bonnet string. There are other ways to sign for "girl." In this book, we will use more modern signs whenever possible to be as representative and inclusive as possible, as opposed to relying on more old-fashioned or outdated transla-tions. As mentioned, signs can change throughout time. If you've learned a sign and see a different interpretation of it, it doesn't mean you are wrong; you may just be seeing a variation of the sign/vocabulary. Also, although the reference or visual cue of a sign may vary, it doesn't change the word's meaning or intent.

THE BUILDING BLOCKS OF SIGNS

ASL employs five parameters for signing. These parameters are all things you'll take into consideration when performing a sign:

1. Handshape
2. Location
3. Movement
4. Palm orientation
5. Nonmanual markers

Here we'll go over each.

Handshape. This is the shape the hand makes while signing. Some handshapes are named after the letter or number they emulate, including the handshapes for A, B, C, O, S, 1, and 5.

Other common handshapes include 3, 2, and bent V. For instance, the difference between RED and CUTE is that RED uses a 1 handshape and CUTE has a 2 handshape.

RED

CUTE

Location. Every sign has a designated place or location to be on or near the body. Locations can be near the chin, forehead, shoulders, right arm, left arm, chest, belly, and so on. For instance, the only difference between MOM and DAD are their locations. MOM is signed at the chin; DAD is signed at the forehead. Some signs start in one location and end in another. Signs can change meaning by simply adding another location.

MOM   **DAD**

Movement. Movement plays a crucial part in ASL. This involves the particular way the arms, hands, and fingers move to produce a sign. A sign can move in many ways: shake, tap, slide, circular, up and down, side to side, back and forth, and more. The movement determines the meaning of the word or words. For instance, with AIRPLANE and FLY, the action of the hands can change a word from a noun (AIRPLANE) to a verb (FLY).

AIRPLANE   **FLY**

Palm Orientation. This describes the way the palm is facing. Palm orientation can be inward (toward the body), facing down, facing up, and outward (away from the body). Some signs may change orientation in the middle or at the end of a word. These changes can alter the meaning of the word or words, such as MINE and YOURS, which are distinguished from each other by a change in **palm orientation.**

MINE   **YOURS**

Nonmanual Markers (NMM). A nonmanual marker refers to head positions (tilting, raising, etc.), body language, and facial expressions (mouth morphemes also known as mouthing, eyebrow movement, and eye movement). These additional elements help convey grammatical information, especially with Wh- questions (who, **what, where, when, why, which, and how) and yes/no questions. Some signs, such as UNDERSTAND and DON'T-UNDERSTAND (page 11), are the same, except for the NMM, which changes the meaning.**

In order for an ASL sign to convey the meaning you want, each parameter must be used correctly. If any of the parameters are off, the meaning of the word may change. The precision of the signs is important to ensure the message is clear to the receiver.

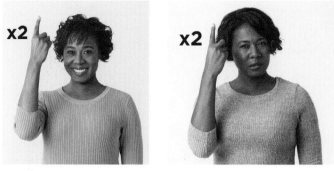

UNDERSTAND **DON'T-UNDERSTAND**

FACIAL EXPRESSIONS

Facial expressions are an important aspect of ASL. Deaf people rely on facial cues to help identify emotions and grammar. When using facial expressions, it's important to match the signs you are using. Altering a person's facial expression can change the meaning of the word or phrase. For instance, the difference between MAD and FURIOUS depends on the facial expression.

In the hearing world, people use vocal inflection to understand the emotion being conveyed in words and/or phrases. Facial expressions play a similar role in ASL and Deaf or hard of hearing communities.

WH- EXPRESSIONS

Along with facial expressions, a person lifting or lowering their eyebrows can also determine what type of question a person may be asking. For example, if the eyebrows are raised, it is to be assumed they are asking a yes or no question, but if the eyebrows are lowered, it is assumed they are asking a Wh- question (who, what, where, when, why, how).

It can be helpful to practice facial expressions in front of a mirror.

FINGERSPELLING

Like many other languages, the words in ASL are made with letters from the alphabet. ASL uses fingerspelling, which means using specific handshapes to create letters that spell out English words. Most English words have an ASL sign, but there are many instances where words don't have specific signs. In these cases, fingerspelling is used. Fingerspelling is commonly used for names, titles, and places.

WH- QUESTIONS

WHO?

WHAT?

WHERE?

WHEN?

WHICH?

WHY?

HOW?

A few tips when fingerspelling:

- Keep your hand in the shoulder/chest region.
- Don't bounce your hand, unless you're spelling double consecutive letters in a word.
- Ensure your palm is facing the receiver, unless you're fingerspelling the letters that face inward (G and H).
- Don't worry about speed; focus on accuracy.
- When fingerspelling two words, pause between the first and second word, then continue. This pause represents the space.

Here are three options for fingerspelling double consecutive letters in a word:

Slide: Move your hand in a small sliding movement.

Bounce: Gently bounce your hand.

Hold/pause: Pause for a short period to hold the letter in place.

Fingerspelling is a method many people use to ask how to sign a particular word or phrase. Instead, if possible, try to act out or gesture the words or phrases to keep from fingerspelling every time.

DOMINANT HAND

"Which hand do I sign with?" is one of the common questions when beginning ASL. It's easy: Use your dominant hand as the primary hand when fingerspelling or signing a phrase. The nondominant hand is considered the supporting hand.

As you learn, keep the signer's perspective in mind. In this case, the model pictured in this book is right-handed, so if you are right-handed, you will be producing the signs in reverse. If you are left-handed, then you make the signs as if you are looking at yourself in a mirror. Don't switch hands as you are signing, as this may confuse the message being received or become a distraction. Practicing in front of a mirror or video-recording yourself are great ways to help become self-aware and build the habit of not switching your hands during a conversation.

OTHER INSTRUCTIONS

We've talked a bit about guidelines for effectively forming letters and words. Now let's explore a few other rules of ASL.

SENTENCE STRUCTURE

There are a few different sentence structure formats; that is, how a sentence is formed. One common format used in ASL is the "Topic, Comment" sentence structure. This structure starts with signing the topic or main idea of the sentence, then follows with the rest of the information in the sentence. Take the English sentence "I want a new car." When we look at the rules for Topic, Comment structure, we see that "car" is the topic or main idea of the sentence, so this would go first, then we would add the rest of the information of the sentence as follows: "CAR NEW I WANT." (New is placed after car because it describes the car.)

Another commonly used ASL format is the "Time, Topic, Comment" structure. This structure focuses mainly on the tense, or time frame. In this format, the tense goes at the beginning of the sentence, followed by the topic and comment. Let's look at the English sentence "I went to the store yesterday." In ASL, "yesterday" represents the tense or time frame, so it goes first. Next, look for the topic; in this case, "store." Finally, you'd address the comment, also known as the predicate, "I went to" (which would be translated to "I go to finish"). All together, the ASL sentence would be "YESTERDAY STORE I GO TO FINISH." One more thing: Since this particular sentence has the word "yesterday," past tense is already implied, so you don't actually need "finish." If the sentence had simply read "I went to the store," the word "finish" would need to be included to convey past tense.

This is a lot of information, for sure. But you'll catch on!

TENSES

In ASL, there are three common ways to represent tenses within a sentence. Read the following guidelines to help you understand how you can express a time frame in a sentence.

1. If you are using the Time, Topic, Comment sentence structure, your tense will generally follow the time established in the sentence (yesterday, tomorrow, next year, two months ago, last year, before, etc.). This allows the receiver to understand specifically when the topic took place.

2. You can establish tense after the verb in the sentence to identify if it has happened or will happen. You'll do this using either FINISH or WILL signs. Two examples: 1) Verb + Finish = have done (or completed) or 2) Verb + Will = will happen (not yet done). For example:

- **GO-TO + FINISH = WENT-TO**

- **SEE + FINISH = SAW**

- **PLAY + WILL = WILL PLAY**

3. You can use ASL signs such as FINISH (past), NOW (present), and WILL (future). These can typically go either at the end of the sentence or after the verb in the sentence. For example, to translate "I will go to the store," you'd sign: STORE GO-TO I WILL. To translate "I saw my friend," you'd sign: MY FRIEND I SEE FINISH. For "I'm going to bed now," you'd sign: BED I GO-TO NOW.

TYPES OF VERBS

In ASL, we have three different types of verbs: plain verbs, indicating verbs, and depicting verbs. Verbs express an action taking place, an event, or a state of being.

Plain Verbs: In ASL, these are considered normal verbs. To use these verbs, the signer must also identify the subject and the object. Some examples include eat, play, sing, talk, and run.

Indicating Verbs: These are also known as directional verbs and locative verbs. The signer integrates the subject into the verb to create one sign by using a single motion or movement to show the action. Some examples of indicating verbs include give, send, pay, and tell.

Depicting Verbs: Depicting verbs are commonly used with "classifiers" in ASL. Classifiers are handshapes used to help expand on nouns and verbs by giving more descriptive information about movement, shape, size, and location. A deep knowledge of classifiers isn't necessary for beginning ASL, but if you wish to learn more, an ASL class is a great place to start.

CHAPTER 2

THE BASICS:
ABCs, 123s & Beyond

Let's begin signing! In this chapter, we'll start with the basics of ASL: fingerspelling and numbers. It's important to sign the letters, words, and numbers exactly as they appear in the photos. To build a strong foundation of fingerspelling, I recommend practicing thirty minutes each day if possible. While practicing your expressive skills (expressing or producing signs), it's also critical to practice your receptive skills (receiving, or watching with your eyes). At the end of this chapter, two lessons will give you the opportunity to practice with real-world scenarios to help develop your signing skills.

AMERICAN SIGN LANGUAGE MADE EASY FOR BEGINNERS

VOCABULARY: THE ASL ALPHABET

Each letter of the alphabet has a specific handshape form. Pay close attention to each of the letters you sign. Find opportunities to practice fingerspelling as often as you possibly can! I like to use everyday items at home to practice signing. For example, if I see a coffee can, I sign the brand name of the coffee. Here's another tip: When learning the alphabet in ASL, sing along as you sign the alphabet.

An important note to remember when fingerspelling the letters G and H: both letters should be signed with the palm facing inward.

LESSON 2.1: FINGERSPELLING FIRST NAMES PRACTICE

Signs Involved: Letters A–Z

Instructions: In this first lesson, practice fingerspelling the following first names. Remember to keep your hand in front of your shoulder region as you sign. Use smooth motions to produce the letters, with no bouncing or shaking of your hand.

Patrick	Fred	Cherie
Kaitlyn	Rafaela	Trey
Travis	Rogelio	Chelsea
Emily	Tessa	Donovan
Shawn	Meghan	Jacque
Alayah	Zack	Braxton

LESSON 2.2: FINGERSPELLING FIRST AND LAST NAMES PRACTICE

Signs Involved: Letters A–Z

Instructions: In this lesson, practice fingerspelling first and last names. Remember to pause fingerspelling in between the first and last name to show the separation of words.

Thomas Gallaudet	Andrew Foster
Laurent Clerc	Helen Keller
Marlee Matlin	Claudia Gordon

CULTURAL DISCUSSION: NAME SIGNS

Every language and culture throughout the world uses names to identify people. Likewise, Deaf and hard of hearing people use fingerspelling to sign a person's name or "name sign" in conversations. Name signs are a unique, personal way to identify someone without having to fully fingerspell their name. Name signs are created by Deaf individuals for members of the Deaf community.

There are two types of name signs: arbitrary and descriptive. Arbitrary name signs are common signs, such as the initials of the person's first and last name. Descriptive name signs are based upon the characteristics or features of a person, such as body movement or personality. A name sign is important and valued within the Deaf and hard of hearing communities.

TIP: When fingerspelling double letters (like the two Ls in Keller), you can slide, double-bounce, or hold each letter slightly longer. See page 13 for more details.

VOCABULARY: NUMBER PRACTICE

In this section, you'll learn how to sign numbers in ASL. We'll cover numbers 1 to 30, then 40, 50, 60, 70, 80, 90, 100, and the signs for thousand and million. In ASL, we typically use one hand to sign numbers, though in some cases, the supporting hand is used to help sign the larger numbers.

When counting the numbers 1 to 5, your palm faces toward you. When signing numbers 6 to 9, a good way to remember which finger to use is to note that the pinkie is the smallest number starting with 6, then as the finger gets bigger, the number gets bigger: ring finger = 7, middle finger = 8, index finger = 9.

1   2   3   4   5

6   7   8   9   10

11

12

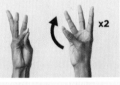

13

14   15   16

CONTINUED →

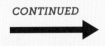

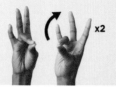

17

18

19

20

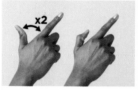

21

22

23

24

25

26

27

28

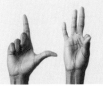

29

30

40

50

60

70

80

90

100

1 THOUSAND

1 MILLION

LESSON 2.3: COUNT ON IT

Signs Involved: Numbers

Instructions: When signing larger numbers, we use the sign for "thousand" and "million" as if they represent the comma in the numbers. For example, when signing 2,000, sign the number 2 and then sign for thousand. After completing this lesson, practice signing mixed numbers; for example, 4,350. To sign this, you would sign the number 4, the sign for thousand, 3 hundred (the number 3, then the letter C; see tip on this page), then 50.

Apply your learning of numbers from pages 21 to 23 to sign the following numbers. Refer back to those pages to review the signs for numbers before continuing and as needed. Remember to count numbers 1 to 5 with your palm facing toward you.

TIP: When signing 100s, the letter C represents 00. For instance, 1C = 100. You will sign this by making a 1 and then a C. Likewise, 300 would be represented by a 3 and then a C. For signed numbers in the thousands, sign the first number and then the sign for thousand.

Count by 1s
1, 2, 3, 4, 5, 6, 7, 8, 9, 10

Count by 10s
10, 20, 30, 40, 50, 60, 70, 80, 90

Count by 100s
100, 200, 300, 400, 500, 600, 700, 800, 900

Count by 1,000s
1,000; 2,000; 3,000; 4,000; 5,000; 6,000; 7,000; 8,000; 9,000

Additional Numbers
10,000; 100,000; 500,000; 1,000,000

LESSON 2.4: PHONE NUMBERS

Signs Involved: Numbers

Instructions: Using your knowledge of numbers, practice signing phone numbers. When signing phone numbers, your palm always faces away from you. After you have completed this lesson, practice signing your and your family's phone numbers.

1. 877-293-4820
2. 817-298-7891
3. 918-392-0156
4. 798-234-8741
5. 904-102-1156

6. 940-194-6532
7. 588-342-1124
8. 214-765-4398
9. 705-431-0043
10. 394-489-5503

My phone number: _____

My father's/mother's number: _____

My friend's number: _____

CHAPTER 3

GREETINGS & PEOPLE

Let's get social! In this chapter, you'll learn how to use ASL to greet people and signs for pronouns/referents, interrogations, and family. You will learn a few different types of simple greetings as well as how to introduce yourself. In addition, in our ongoing discussion on Deaf culture, you'll learn about the customs of getting a Deaf person's attention.

HELLO

Make a flat open handshape with your dominant hand. Touch the side of the index finger to the side of your forehead and bring your hand up and out as if saluting.

I/ME

Make a 1 handshape with your dominant hand and point to your chest.

MY/MINE

Make a flat handshape with your dominant hand and touch your palm to your chest.

NAME

With both hands in U handshapes, fingers pointing forward, tap the two fingers of your dominant hand against the two fingers of your nondominant hand two times.

YOUR/YOURS/THEIRS

To sign YOUR or YOURS, hold up your dominant hand in a flat open handshape with the fingers pointed up. Point the palm in the direction of the person you are talking about.

To sign THEIRS, sweep the hand in the YOUR position to the side to show plural. Refer to the signing tip for YOU (page 30) for instructions on how to refer to people who are not present. In ASL, pronouns are not gender-specific.

THANK-YOU/YOU'RE-WELCOME

Make a flat open handshape with your dominant hand, palm facing inward. Touch your fingertips to your mouth/chin area and move your hand forward without reversing the palm.

TIP: If someone signs THANK-YOU to you, you simply sign THANK-YOU right back at them to communicate YOU'RE-WELCOME.

YOU/HE/SHE/IT

Make a 1 handshape with your dominant hand and point toward the person you are referring to. If you are talking about yourself, point to your chest.

TIP: When referring to people who are not present, first communicate who you are talking about, then establish a reference point for them by pointing slightly downward at a spot in the space in front of you. Continue to refer to that same spot for any ongoing pronouns related to that non-present individual. Once the topic changes, new reference points can be established for new characters.

THEMSELVES

Make an A handshape with your dominant hand, thumb pointing upward and palm facing to the side. Push your fist forward two times in the direction of whomever you are referring to. If you are referencing more than one person, sweep the hand sideways while making this sign.

TIP: See the signing tip for YOU (above) for instructions on how to refer to individuals who are not physically present. Pronouns in ASL are not gender-specific.

YOURSELF

Make an A handshape with your dominant hand, palm facing to the side, and push the fist forward one or two times in the direction of the person you are referring to.

TIP: Refer to the signing tip for YOU (page 30) for instructions on how to refer to people who are not present. In ASL, pronouns are not gender-specific.

TWO-OF-US

Make a 2 handshape with your dominant hand held in front of the body, palm facing up. Move your hand back and forth, alternating between pointing your index finger at the person you are referring to and pointing your middle finger toward yourself.

OURS

Make a flat handshape with your dominant hand. Touch the side of the hand to your dominant shoulder, then circle the hand in front of the body in an arch, palm facing toward you, until the other side of the hand touches the other shoulder.

THEY/THEM

Use the index finger of your dominant hand to point at the person you are referring to. If you are referring to more than one person, then sweep the hand sideways while pointing.

TIP: Refer to the signing tip for YOU (page 30) for instructions on how to refer to individuals who are not physically present. Pronouns in ASL are not gender-specific.

NICE/CLEAN

Hold out your nondominant hand in a flat handshape, palm facing up. With your dominant hand also in a flat handshape, wipe your palm across the palm of your nondominant hand, moving away from the body.

TIP: Think of wiping a whiteboard clean.

MEET-YOU

Make 1 handshapes with both hands, your nondominant hand facing inward and your dominant hand facing outward. The hands start apart from each other and come together with the knuckles of both hands touching.

TIP: Imagine that your index fingers are two people coming together face-to-face.

PLEASE

Make a flat open handshape with your dominant hand. Place the palm on your chest and move it in circles two times.

US/WE

Make a 1 handshape with your dominant hand, palm facing inward. Touch the index finger to your dominant shoulder, then arch your finger across to land on your nondominant shoulder.

WHAT?

With both hands in relaxed 5 handshapes, palms facing up, shake your hands side to side while furrowing your eyebrows and tilting your head slightly to the side.

WHAT'S-UP?

With one or both hands in 5 handshapes, palms facing inward and middle fingers extended, touch both middle fingers to the sides of your chest. Move the hands upward while rotating the palms to face upward.

TIP: Your facial expression communicates the energy behind this question. Are you perhaps suspicious, curious, concerned, or just using the sign as a friendly greeting? Show it with your face.

WELCOME

Hold out your dominant hand away from the body in a flat handshape, palm facing inward, and bring the hand in toward your torso.

TIP: The WELCOME concept of this sign refers to the greeting, not YOU'RE WELCOME (page 29).

SEE-YOU-LATER

Make an L handshape with your dominant hand and touch the thumb next to your eye on the same side of the body. Move the hand forward, away from your face, as the hand arches downward.

TIP: This is almost the same as the sign for LATER, but it initiates next to the eye to indicate SEE.

PERSON

Hold out both hands in flat open handshapes, palms facing each other but several inches apart. Move both hands straight down several inches while maintaining the handshapes and palm orientation.

TIP: Think of drawing the vertical position of an upright human.

BOY

With your dominant hand in front of your forehead, make a pinching movement with all of the fingers while moving your hand away from your forehead.

TIP: Think of pulling on the rim of a baseball cap.

GIRL

Make an A handshape with your dominant hand and brush the tip of the thumb down the dominant side of your jawline.

TIP: Think of a curl of hair framing the chin.

MOM

Make a 5 handshape with your dominant hand, palm facing to the side. Touch the tip of the thumb to your chin or tap it on your chin slightly two times.

DAD

Make a 5 handshape with your dominant hand, palm facing to the side. Touch the tip of the thumb to your forehead or tap it on your forehead slightly two times.

TIP: The upper part of the face is the reference point for male referents.

GRANDPA/GREAT-GRANDPA

To sign GRANDPA, make a 5 handshape with your dominant hand, palm facing to the side. Touch your thumb to your forehead, then move your hand forward, away from your face, in one or two arching movements.

Add another arching movement to communicate GREAT-GRANDPA.

GRANDMA/GREAT-GRANDMA

To sign GRANDMA, make a 5 handshape with your dominant hand, palm facing to the side. Touch your thumb to your chin, then move your hand forward, away from your face, in one or two arching movements.

Add another arching movement to communicate GREAT-GRANDMA.

UNCLE

Hold your dominant hand in a U handshape, palm facing outward. Hold it near the side of your forehead, but not touching your face. Make small circular or shaking motions with the hand.

AUNT

Make an A handshape with your dominant hand, palm facing outward. Hold it near the side of your cheek next to your chin, but not touching your face, and make two small circling or twisting motions with the hand.

SISTER

Hold your nondominant hand in front of your body in an L handshape, palm facing inward. Make an A or L handshape with your dominant hand and place the thumb on the cheek, near the mouth (female reference). Bring your dominant hand down on top of your nondominant hand, shifting into an L handshape as it lands.

BROTHER

Make an L handshape with your nondominant hand, palm facing to the side or inward, and hold it in front of your body. Make an A or L handshape with your dominant hand, placing the thumb at the side of the forehead. Bring your dominant hand down on top of your nondominant hand, making an L handshape as it lands.

COUSIN

Make a C handshape with your dominant hand near the side of your face, palm facing inward, and wiggle the hand two times.

TIP: You can indicate a male cousin by making this sign by the upper part of your face. You can indicate a female cousin by making the sign by the lower part of your face. To make the sign gender-neutral, sign it by the center of your face.

CHILD/CHILDREN

To sign CHILD, use just the dominant hand, lowering it down once as if resting your hand on the head of a small child.

For CHILDREN, make flat B handshapes in front of the body with both hands, palms down. Make a downward tapping motion with both hands, then bounce your hands farther apart and tap downward again.

DAUGHTER

Make flat B handshapes with both hands. Position your nondominant hand in front of your body, palm facing up, as if holding a baby. With the fingers of your dominant hand, touch the side of your face near the chin (female reference), then drop the hand down until it rests in the crook of your nondominant elbow with the palm facing up.

SON

Make flat B handshapes with both hands. Hold your nondominant hand up in front of your body, palm facing up, as if holding a baby. With your dominant hand, palm facing down, touch the side of your forehead (male reference), then bring the hand down on top of the nondominant arm, palm facing up.

DEAF

Make a 1 handshape with your dominant hand, palm facing outward, and touch your index finger to the side of your chin. Move the finger away from your chin and touch the back of your jaw.

TIP: You will also see this signed with the finger starting at the back of the jaw and ending on the chin.

HEARING

Make a 1 handshape with your dominant hand, with the index finger held horizontally in front of the lips. Circle the finger away from the lips two times.

TIP: The finger circles out from your mouth as if words were spilling out of your mouth from talking.

FAMILY

With both hands in F hand-shapes, palms facing outward and the tips of your thumbs and index fingers pinched together in front of your body, rotate your hands around until your pinkie fingers touch and your palms are facing inward.

FATHER-IN-LAW

This sign is a combination of DAD (page 36) and LAW. First, sign DAD with your dominant hand in the 5 handshape, palm facing to the side. Touch the tip of the thumb to your forehead or tap it on your forehead slightly two times. Sign LAW by holding your nondominant hand in a flat handshape, palm facing to the side or upward. Make an L handshape with your dominant hand, palm facing the other hand. Tap the dominant hand once on the top of the palm of your other hand, then tap again once more at the bottom.

MOTHER-IN-LAW

This sign is a combination of MOM (page 36) and LAW. First, sign MOM with your dominant hand in the 5 handshape, palm facing to the side. Touch the tip of the thumb to your chin or tap it on your chin slightly two times, then smoothly transition to sign LAW. Sign LAW by holding your nondominant hand in a flat handshape, palm facing to the side or upward. Make an L handshape with your dominant hand, palm facing the other hand. Tap the dominant hand once on the top of the palm of your other hand, then tap again once more at the bottom.

FRIEND/BEST-FRIEND

To sign FRIEND, with both hands in X handshapes, the palm of your nondominant hand facing up and the palm of your dominant hand facing down, hook your index fingers together briefly and then flip your hands so that your dominant hand is now facing up and the nondominant hand is facing down, again hooking your index fingers together briefly.

If you hook your index fingers together and move both hands forward firmly, rather than reversing positions, you are communicating CLOSE or BEST-FRIEND.

HARD-OF-HEARING

Hold your dominant hand in front of your body in an H handshape, palm facing to the side, and tap the hand downward two times toward imaginary spots that are side by side.

TIP: HH is the abbreviation for hard of hearing.

HUSBAND

Make relaxed C handshapes with both hands, the palm of your nondominant hand facing up and the palm of your dominant hand facing down. Touch the thumb of your dominant hand to the side of your forehead (male reference), then bring it down to clasp your nondominant hand, which is the sign for MARRIED (page 170).

WIFE

Make relaxed C handshapes with both hands, the palm of your nondominant hand facing up and the palm of your dominant hand facing down. Touch the fingers of your dominant hand to the lower side of your face (female reference), then bring it down to clasp your nondominant hand, which is the sign for MARRIED (page 170).

MAN

Make a 5 handshape with your dominant hand, palm facing to the side. Touch the thumb to your forehead (male reference), then bring the hand down and touch the thumb to the center of your chest.

TIP: WOMAN (below) is communicated by making the same sign but while touching the lower part of the face (female reference).

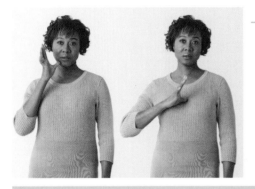

WOMAN

Make a 5 handshape with your dominant hand, palm facing to the side. Touch the thumb to your chin (female reference), then bring the hand down and touch the thumb to the center of your chest.

TIP: MAN (above) is communicated by making the same sign but while touching the upper part of the face (male reference).

LESSON 3.1: GREETINGS & PEOPLE

Signs Involved: Greetings, polite phrases, pronouns/referents, interrogations, people/family

Instructions: Read the following English sentences and their ASL translations. Practice signing each ASL translation. Use the vocabulary from chapter 2 and this chapter to help you practice these sentences. Once you practice signing the sentences, video-record yourself so you can review how you are signing.

Remember that when signing a Wh- word (who, what, where, when, why, which, and how), lower your eyebrows to indicate a question is being asked.

HELLO   **MY**   **NAME**

English Sentence: Hello, my name is _____.

ASL Translation: HELLO I/ME/MY NAME (fingerspell your name)

NAME   **YOURS**   **WHAT?**

English Sentence: What is your name?

ASL Translation: NAME YOURS WHAT?

NICE　　　　**MEET-YOU**

English Sentence: Nice to meet you.

ASL Translation: NICE MEET-YOU

SEE-YOU-LATER

English Sentence: I'll see you later.

ASL Translation: SEE-YOU-LATER

CULTURAL DISCUSSION: GETTING A DEAF PERSON'S ATTENTION

There are several methods for getting a Deaf person's attention. A few common ways would be by stomping on the floor, flashing the room lights, waving your hand in the air toward the person, or tapping on their shoulder. Although some of these differ from the hearing way of getting someone's attention and might even seem strange or off-putting, these methods are acceptable and can be used in almost any situation.

LESSON 3.2: FAMILY TREE

Signs Involved: Family signs (grandfather, grandmother, dad, mom, brother, sister, uncle, aunt, cousin [male and female], niece, nephew), fingerspelling

Instructions: In this lesson, you'll be creating a family tree. Feel free to choose which family members you would like to include. Before continuing on to this lesson, you'll want to review the vocabulary for family signs. Use the ten spaces provided to write in each family member's role and their names. Not all spaces need to be filled in. Next, sign each family member's role (father, mother, sister, etc.), then fingerspell their names. Be as creative as you'd like. Challenge yourself to use your family members' full names. Practice in front of a mirror or video-record yourself to watch how you are signing the vocabulary and fingerspelling the names.

Signing Sample

Family member: Father **Name:** Robert

Family member: Mother **Name:** McKenzie

Family member: Sister **Name:** Madison

Family member: Brother **Name:** Benjamin

My Family Tree

Family member: _____ Family member: _____
Name: _____ Name: _____

Family member: _____ Family member: _____
Name: _____ Name: _____

Family member: _____ Family member: _____
Name: _____ Name: _____

Family member: _____ Family member: _____
Name: _____ Name: _____

Family member: _____ Family member: _____
Name: _____ Name: _____

TIP: To help remember how to distinguish male and female signs, picture an imaginary horizontal line across the middle of your face. From the nose to the forehead, you will see male signs, such as dad, grandpa, uncle, brother, etc. From the nose down to your chin, you will see female signs, such as mom, sister, grandma, aunt, etc.

LESSON 3.3: CHAPTER 3 VOCABULARY QUIZ

Signs Involved: Greetings and people

Instructions: This multiple-choice quiz will test your knowledge of the vocabulary you learned in this chapter. Before taking this assessment, feel free to review the vocabulary to familiarize yourself with the signs. Look closely at the pictures and possible answers before responding, as some answers may be similar. Then check your responses against the Answer Key (page 243).

MULTIPLE-CHOICE QUESTIONS

1.

a. Theirs
b. Your/yours
c. Two-of-us
d. Welcome

2.

a. Boy
b. Girl
c. Person
d. Themselves

3.

a. Yourself
b. Mine
c. Ours
d. Hearing

4.

a. Woman
b. Grandpa
c. Man
d. Son

5.

a. Themselves
b. See-you-later
c. They/them
d. Nice/clean

6.

a. Aunt
b. Uncle
c. Girl
d. Cousin

7.

a. Hearing
b. Family
c. Deaf
d. Mom

8.

a. Name
b. You/he/she/it
c. Themselves
d. Two-of-us

9.

a. Theirs
b. Themselves
c. They/them
d. Meet-you

10.

a. Brother
b. Sister
c. Girl
d. Boy

11.

a. Mother-in-law
b. Father-in-law
c. Mother
d. Father

12.

a. Wife
b. Husband
c. Hard-of-hearing
d. Deaf

13.

a. I/me
b. My/mine
c. Your/yours
d. Hello

14.

a. Daughter
b. Son
c. Child/
   children
d. Family

15.

a. Family
b. Cousin
c. Friend
d. Woman

CHAPTER 4

THOUGHTS & FEELINGS

In this chapter, you'll be introduced to signs on thoughts and feelings. Although we'll focus on beginner ASL signs, signs expressing thoughts and feelings can be the most difficult to sign. This is because, in addition to the hand movements, facial expressions and body language also play a crucial role in expressing linguistic information and emotions, similar to vocal inflections in English. This chapter will help you gain experience practicing your facial expressions and body language. As you practice each sign, think of various scenarios in which you might use them. Don't worry about looking silly—the sillier you look, the better—because silliness means you're expressing the message or emotion clearly.

AFRAID/SCARED

With both hands in 5 handshapes in front of your chest, palms facing inward and fingertips pointing at each other, move your hands quickly toward each other and back again one or more times.

ANGRY/GRUMPY/MAD

To sign ANGRY or MAD, make a 5 handshape with your dominant hand in front of your face, palm facing inward, then stiffen and bend your fingers into a 5-claw handshape.

GRUMPY is done by flexing the fingers a couple of times while making this sign.

TIP: Intensity of facial expression and sign movement is what shows different degrees of the emotion of anger. The stronger the expression and/or sign movement, the stronger the emotion.

NOT/DON'T

Make an A handshape with your dominant hand, palm facing to the side. Place the thumb under your chin and bring it forward, away from your body, in a swift movement.

TIP: Many of the negative signs push away from the body, as if distancing the signer from an unwanted object.

BAWL/SOB

With both hands held horizontally in 4 handshapes, palms facing inward and the tips of your index fingers under your eyes, trace two or three lines down the face as if multiple tears are falling.

TIP: Make sure you have a very anguished look on your face.

BORED

Touch the index finger of your dominant hand to the side of your nose and make a twisting motion. You can also make this sign bigger for emphasis.

BRAVE/CONFIDENT/HEALTHY

With both hands in 5 handshapes, touch both hands to your shoulders, then pull them away from your shoulders and close your hands into fists.

TIP: For BRAVE and CONFIDENT, the hands tend to move out to the sides; for HEALTHY, they tend to move forward, in front of the body.

CONCERN

With both hands in 5 handshapes, palms facing inward and the middle fingers extended forward, tap the middle fingers alternately to your upper chest.

TIP: It's helpful to show a concerned expression on your face along with this sign.

CONFUSED

With both hands in claw handshapes near your forehead, palms facing each other, make rotating, circular motions with both hands while keeping the palms facing each other.

TIP: People often point to the side of their forehead before they do this sign, almost like communicating "brain fog."

CRAZY

Make a claw handshape with your dominant hand and hold it to the side of your face, a few inches away. Make a twisting movement with your wrist two times.

CURIOUS

With your dominant hand, pinch a bit of the skin on the front of your neck with the thumb and index finger and twist the hand slightly a couple of times.

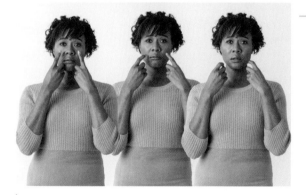

CRY

With both hands in 1 handshapes, palms facing inward, touch your fingertips to your cheeks just under the eyes. Drag your index fingers down your cheeks like tears falling.

DEPRESSED

With both hands in 5 handshapes and middle fingers extended forward, touch the middle fingers to each respective side of the body, just inside the shoulder blades. Slide both hands downward.

TIP: Think of the downward movement past the heart representing "feeling down."

DISAPPOINTED/MISS-YOU

For DISAPPOINTED, make a 1 handshape with your dominant hand, palm facing inward, and hold the tip of your index finger to your chin while making a disappointed expression.

The sign for MISS-YOU is the same, but your face takes on a more sorrowful expression.

EMBARRASSED

With both hands in 5 handshapes, hold both palms close to your cheeks and alternately move them upward in circular movements.

TIP: Think of red flushed cheeks from feeling embarrassed. There are several other ways to sign this word. Defer to your local Deaf community.

ENJOY

With both hands in flat open handshapes, palms facing inward, place your dominant hand on your chest and your nondominant hand on your stomach. Circle your hands, with your dominant hand circling clockwise and your nondominant hand circling counterclockwise.

EXCITED/THRILLED/EVENT

To sign EXCITED, with both hands in 5 handshapes, palms facing inward and middle finger extended forward, alternately brush your middle fingers up the sides of your chest in a circular motion two times.

If you move both hands upward simultaneously one time, you are communicating THRILLED or EVENT.

TIP: To picture this movement, think of lots of happy feelings jumping around in your body.

FACIAL-EXPRESSION

Make X handshapes with both hands and position them next to each side of your face, palms facing your face, and move them up and down a couple of times.

TIP: Think of holding puppet strings connected to your face that control your expressions.

FEEL

Make a 5 handshape with your dominant hand and extend the middle finger forward. Touch the extended middle finger to the center of your chest and make two upward stroking movements.

FRIENDLY

Make 5 handshapes with both hands and position them next to your cheeks. Move the hands backward and out to the sides while wiggling your fingers.

TIP: This can also be used to communicate a pleasant or charismatic disposition.

FUNNY

Make a U handshape with your dominant hand, and brush the two fingertips up and down the tip of your nose two times.

HAPPY

Make a flat open handshape with your dominant hand, palm facing inward, and brush your hand up your chest in a circular motion two times.

TIP: A smile typically accompanies this sign, unless you want to show sarcasm, which would be communicated if you frowned while signing HAPPY.

INSPIRED

Hold both hands in flat O handshapes to the middle of your chest, palms facing inward. Move both hands upward while opening the hands into 5 handshapes.

LAZY

Make an L handshape with your dominant hand, and slap the palm on your opposite shoulder two times.

TIP: An uncaring facial expression typically accompanies this sign.

LOVE/HUG

To sign LOVE, with both hands in fists, cross your arms and touch the fists to the opposite shoulders, like a bear hug.

If you hold the sign longer and shake the body a bit, this indicates HUG.

LOVE-IT (KISS-FIST)

Make an S handshape with your dominant hand, palm facing outward. Place the back of the hand on your lips as if you are kissing it, then push the hand forward in a quick movement.

TIP: This sign for love is typically used to refer to nonromantic preferences, such as "I love that new restaurant," "I love reading," or "I love the new teacher."

MISCHIEVOUS/NAUGHTY

Make a 3 handshape with your dominant hand. Touch the thumb to the side of your forehead and bend the other two fingers a few times.

TIP: A sneaky expression goes well with this sign.

NERVOUS

With both hands in 5 handshapes in front of your body, palms facing down, shake your hands as if you were very jittery.

TIP: Think of your hands shaking as though you had one too many cups of coffee.

PATIENCE/SUFFER

Make an A handshape with your dominant hand. Touch the back of the thumb to the front of your mouth and pull the hand downward past your chin.

TIP: A facial expression to communicate your level of patience or suffering helps distinguish which emotion you are expressing and its level.

PITY/MERCY/FEEL-SORRY-FOR

Hold out your dominant hand in a 5 handshape, palm facing down, and extend the middle finger slightly farther than the others. Move the hand in a circular motion with a sympathetic facial expression.

TIP: You can also do this sign with two hands for emphasis.

PRESSURE/STRESS

Make an S handshape with your nondominant hand, palm facing to the side, and make a 5 handshape with your dominant hand. Rest your dominant hand on top of the S handshape. Push your nondominant hand downward two times with your dominant hand.

TIP: Think of a bottle being pressurized again and again that will explode at any minute.

PROUD

Make an A handshape with your dominant hand, palm facing down, and touch your thumb to your belly button area, then pull it straight up to the top of your chest.

TIP: Think of zipping up a uniform that you are proud to wear.

RUDE/MEAN

Hold out your nondominant hand in a flat handshape, palm facing up. With your dominant hand also in a flat handshape, extend the middle finger forward to touch it to your nondominant palm and slide it from the heel of the hand past the fingertips. This communicates RUDE.

If you make a claw handshape with the dominant hand and make the same movement, you can communicate MEAN (as in not nice).

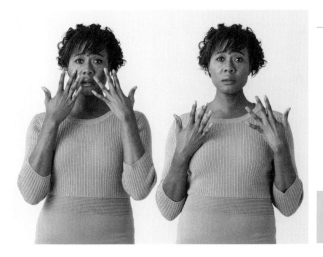

SAD

With both hands in front of your face in 5 handshapes, palms facing inward, pull both hands straight down several inches.

TIP: A sad expression accompanies this sign.

SENSITIVE/INSENSITIVE

To sign SENSITIVE, make a 5 handshape in front of your chest with your dominant hand, touch your middle finger to your heart area, and twist the wrist downward two times.

To communicate INSEN-SITIVE, add the sign for NOT (page 55): Make an open A handshape with your dominant hand, palm facing to the side. Place the thumb under the chin and bring it forward, away from your body, in a swift movement.

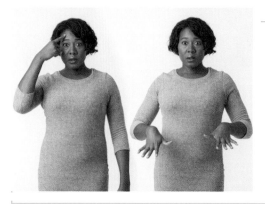

SHOCKED

Make a 1 handshape with your dominant hand, palm facing inward. Touch the index finger to the side of your forehead, then shift both hands into 5 or claw handshapes, fingers facing down, in a downward drop.

TIP: A shocked facial expression is an important nonmanual marker to accompany this sign. There are several other ways to sign SHOCKED. Defer to your local Deaf community.

SHY

Hold up your dominant hand in a loose A handshape, palm facing down, and touch your knuckles to your cheek, then rotate the hand so that the palm faces behind you.

SILLY/GOOFY/RIDICULOUS

Hold a Y handshape in front of your nose, palm facing to the side, and twist your wrist back and forth. This is SILLY or GOOFY.

   To sign RIDICULOUS, make only one large movement with the Y handshape rather than a repeated movement.

STRICT

Make a bent V handshape with your dominant hand and touch the side of the index finger knuckle to your nose.

TIP: You can emphasize strictness by using all four bent fingers rather than just two.

STRUGGLE

Make 1 handshapes with both hands and hold up both index fingers, pointing them directly at each other. Move the hands in circular motions at the same time, keeping the fingers pointing at each other.

STUBBORN

Hold up the dominant hand in a flat handshape, palm facing outward, with the thumb touching the side of your forehead. Fold the other fingers down into an A handshape.

TIRED/EXHAUSTED

With both hands in flat bent handshapes, touch the fingertips just inside your shoulder blades and drop the hands down while maintaining contact.

TIP: People often sag their body and shoulders downward while making this sign.

UPSET

Hold your dominant hand in a flat handshape with the palm resting on your stomach. Pull your hand away from your stomach and flip it palm-up, then bring it back in so the side of the hand is now touching the stomach.

WORRIED

With both hands in flat B handshapes in front of your forehead, palms facing each other, move your hands in alternating circles two times.

UNDERSTAND/DON'T-UNDERSTAND

For UNDERSTAND, make a fist with your dominant hand and touch the thumb knuckle to the side of your forehead. Flick your index finger up two times.

To make this DON'T-UNDERSTAND, simply shake your head in negation while signing UNDERSTAND.

TIP: Think of a light bulb turning on in your head from a good idea.

LESSON 4.1: TALKING ABOUT HOW YOU FEEL

Signs Involved: I/me, thoughts, feelings

Instructions: In Deaf culture, asking about a person's thoughts and feelings is a common practice. However, depending on the culture, expressing emotions through words may not be necessary. Sign language is a visual language where one's thoughts and feelings can be more easily seen, through facial expressions and body language. As you work through the lessons, take note of any cultural differences you notice.

In this lesson, we'll start with the basics of matching the facial expression to the vocabulary. Take notes as you sign the vocabulary words; for example, write down any signs that you need to come back to. Watch yourself in a mirror as you produce the sign along with the facial expression to make sure the signs and facial expressions match. Follow the prompt to help you sign the different vocabulary words. After you have signed all the vocabulary words in the list, think of and practice more words you can add to your list.

Signing Sample

English Sentence: I'm shocked.

I/ME   **SHOCKED**   **I/ME**

Signing Prompt: I'm _____.

Happy	Angry	Upset	Nervous
Sad	Tired	Friendly	Patient
Excited	Confused	Stressed	Sensitive
Worried	Silly	Loved	Scared

Think of four additional words you can use to describe your feelings.

_____   _____

_____   _____

Write down the words you need additional practice signing.

_____

TIP: Ask a friend or family member to watch you sign the vocabulary words to make sure your facial expressions match your signs.

LESSON 4.2: HOW TO STATE WHAT YOU'RE NOT FEELING

Signs Involved: Thoughts, feelings, not, adjectives

Instructions: In lesson 4.1, you practiced signing adjectives that express thoughts and feelings. However, in Deaf culture, it's common for Deaf people to ask you if you are feeling a certain way, based on your facial expression or body language. There are times your facial expressions and body language don't convey your true emotions. In instances like this, we can use NOT before or after the adjective to show that we are not, in fact, feeling that way. For example, if somebody asks if you are angry, you can sign that you are not angry.

This lesson will focus on the grammatical structure for expressing how to use NOT when describing your thoughts and feelings. Similar to the grammar structure in lesson 4.1, we will follow the same structure, but this time we'll add NOT. ASL grammar structure allows us to choose to sign NOT either before or after the adjective when expressing emotions.

TIP: Remember to shake your head and use the proper facial expression as you sign about how you feel.

Signing Sample

English Sentence: I am not nervous.

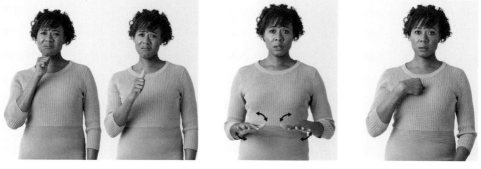

NOT　　　　　　　　　　**NERVOUS**　　　　**I/ME**

The following prompts show how to use NOT when responding to another person. Following one or both prompts, sign each word listed to say you are NOT feeling a certain way.

Signing Prompt

NOT _____ I. / _____ NOT I.

Use the following list to express that you are not:

Disappointed	Mad	Afraid
Inspired	Embarrassed	Bored
Lazy	Scared	Happy
Mischievous	Upset	Depressed

LESSON 4.3: CLARIFYING HOW YOU FEEL

Signs Involved: I/me, not, thoughts, feelings

Instructions: In the previous lessons, you learned how to express your emotions, as well as how to use NOT when expressing negative statements. When expressing a negative statement, it's important to clarify what you *are* feeling because your facial expressions or body language may contradict your true emotions. This lesson expands your response to add a clarification statement about your thoughts and feelings. Use the following signing sample and prompt to sign the list of emotions.

Signing Sample

English Sentence: I'm not scared; I'm nervous.

ASL Translation: NOT SCARED I/ME; NERVOUS I/ME.

NOT

SCARED

I/ME

NERVOUS

I/ME

Review the vocabulary words from this chapter. Then, using the signing prompt, select one word from the NOT list and one word from the AM list to practice. Repeat until all the words have been signed.

TIP: Remember, you can use NOT either before or after the adjective.

Signing Prompt: NOT _____ I; _____ I.

NOT	AM
Lazy	Inspired
Scared	Angry
Excited	Curious
Disappointed	Embarrassed
Shy	Stressed
Stubborn	Brave
Tired	Happy

CULTURAL DISCUSSION: NEGATIVE STATEMENTS

Since ASL is a visual language, clarifying after the negative statement is an important part of communicating with a Deaf person, because facial expressions and body language can also have different interpretations when you are signing.

LESSON 4.4: CHAPTER 4 VOCABULARY QUIZ

Signs Involved: Family, people, thoughts, feelings

Instructions: This multiple-choice quiz will test your knowledge of the vocabulary you learned in this chapter. Before taking this assessment, feel free to review the vocabulary to familiarize yourself with the signs. Look closely at the pictures and possible answers before responding, as some answers may be similar. Then check your responses against the Answer Key (page 243).

1.

a. Proud
b. Angry
c. Brave
d. Curious

2.

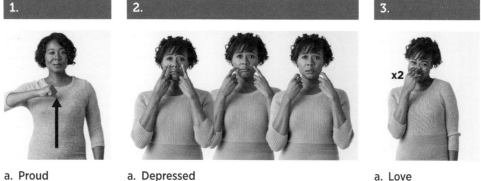

a. Depressed
b. Enjoy
c. Cry
d. Embarrassed

3.

a. Love
b. Funny
c. Nervous
d. Mischievous

4.

a. Angry
b. Bored
c. Lazy
d. Funny

5.

a. Happy
b. Friendly
c. Curious
d. Confident

6.

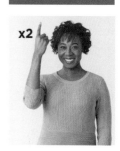

a. Understand
b. Don't-understand
c. Afraid
d. Facial-expression

7.

a. Disappointed
b. Angry
c. Bawl/sob
d. Feel

8.

a. Love-it
b. Depressed
c. Embarrassed
d. Confused

9.

a. Inspired
b. Rude/mean
c. Sensitive
d. Upset

10.

a. Worried
b. Upset
c. Afraid
d. Embarrassed

11.

a. Rude/mean
b. Afraid
c. Struggle
d. Crazy

12.

a. Afraid
b. Stubborn
c. Bored
d. Pity

13.

a. Pity
b. Brave
c. Angry
d. Disappointed

14.

a. Lazy
b. Funny
c. Pity
d. Enjoy

15.

a. Excited
b. Happy
c. Brave
d. Depressed

16.

a. Excited
b. Facial-expression
c. Don't-understand
d. Understand

17.

a. Sensitive
b. Strict
c. Cry
d. Curious

18.

a. Shy
b. Confused
c. Strict
d. Silly

19.

a. Strict
b. Silly
c. Angry
d. Facial-expression

20.

a. Crazy
b. Shocked
c. Curious
d. Depressed

CHAPTER 5

DAILY ROUTINES

In this chapter, you'll be introduced to daily routines, weather, and seasons. When studying this vocabulary, pay close attention to the movements that accompany the signs. Some signs may look similar; however, movement can change the meaning of a word or words. In this chapter, you'll also be learning some verbs. When signing a verb, the movement is repeated to represent it in action. We'll round out this chapter with lessons designed to improve your expressive and receptive skills.

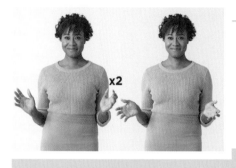

CHAT/TALK

With both hands in claw handshapes held out to the sides, palms angled up, shake both hands downward two times at an inward angle.

TIP: Think of how Deaf people chat with their hands rather than their mouth.

DANCE

Hold out your nondominant hand in a flat open handshape, palm facing up. Make a V handshape with your dominant hand, fingertips pointing down toward the center of your nondominant palm. With your dominant hand above but not touching the palm, move your fingers side to side by twisting your wrist.

TIP: Imagine feet gliding across a dance floor.

EXERCISE/WORKOUT/GYM

With both hands in fists next to your shoulders, palms facing outward, move both arms up and down.

TIP: Think of the action of lifting weights.

FUN

With both hands in U handshapes, position your nondominant hand with the palm facing down. Touch the tips of your two dominant fingers to the tip of your nose, then flip the palm downward and move the two fingers so they land on the back of your two nondominant fingers.

GAME

With both hands in A handshapes, palms facing inward, tap the knuckles of both hands together two times.

HIKE

With both hands in bent 3 handshapes, palms facing down or outward, move the hands forward alternately, mimicking feet taking steps.

MAKE

Make fists with both hands in front of the body and stack one on top of the other. Twist the fists in opposite directions while maintaining contact.

TIP: Think of holding a strip of modeling clay and twisting it to make something out of it.

MOVIE

Make a flat open handshape with your nondominant hand, palm facing inward, and make a 5 handshape with your dominant hand, palm facing outward. Place the dominant hand behind the nondominant hand and shake the dominant hand back and forth twice.

MUSIC/SONG/MUSICIAN

Hold up your nondominant arm, palm facing toward you. With your dominant hand in a flat handshape, thumb pointing upward, wave the hand side to side above your nondominant arm. This is the sign for MUSIC and SONG.

Add the PERSON sign (page 35) after the MUSIC sign to communicate MUSICIAN. Sign PERSON with both hands in flat open handshapes, palms facing each other but several inches apart. Bring your hands straight down several inches while maintaining the handshapes and palm orientation.

PARTY/PLAY

With both hands in Y handshapes, arms held out horizontally in front of the body, move both hands side to side in tandem.

RUN

With both hands in L handshapes, index fingers pointing forward and one hand in front of the other, hook the index finger of the back hand around the thumb of the front hand and wiggle the front index finger as you move the hands forward.

MORNING

With both hands in flat open handshapes, hold up your nondominant arm in front of the body and touch the fingers to the crook of your dominant elbow. Lean the dominant arm forward with the palm facing up, then lift the arm toward you so the palm rises to face you.

SKILL/TALENT

Hold up your nondominant hand in a flat handshape, palm facing to the side. Make a flat handshape with your dominant hand as well. Grab the bottom side of your nondominant hand and pull your dominant hand downward into an A handshape.

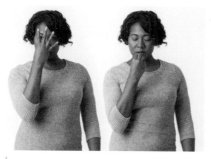

SLEEP/SLEEPY

Hold up your dominant hand in front of your face in a 5 handshape and close the fingers into a flat O handshape as your hand moves downward. This means SLEEP.

If you repeat the movement gently a couple of times with a tired facial expression, this means SLEEPY.

TIP: Think of your eyes closing.

SWIM

This sign is basically a pantomime. Make swim strokes in whatever way you choose.

WALK

With both hands in flat open handshapes in front of your body, palms facing down, alternate moving your hands forward, as if you were taking steps.

WATCH (MOVIE/TV)

Make a bent L handshape with your dominant hand in front of your body, palm facing up. Bring the hand forward in a single motion, as if holding a remote control and aiming it at the receiver.

TIP: This sign for WATCH typically refers to things you watch that are controlled by a remote control.

ALARM

Make a flat handshape in front of your body with your nondominant hand, palm facing outward or to the side. Make a 1 handshape with your dominant hand, and knock the fist against your nondominant palm two times.

TIP: Think of the clanging of a clapper inside of a bell.

APPEARANCE/GOOD-LOOKING/ATTRACTIVE

To sign APPEARANCE, make a 5 handshape with your dominant hand and position it at eye level, palm facing inward. Move your hand in a repeated circular motion.

To communicate GOOD-LOOKING or ATTRACTIVE, sign GOOD before APPEARANCE. To sign GOOD, with both hands in open handshapes, palms facing up, place the tips of the fingers of your dominant hand on your chin. Bring this hand down to land on the palm of the nondominant hand.

BATH

With both hands in A handshapes, palms touching inside your shoulder blades, move your hands up and down simultaneously over your chest.

TIP: This sign looks as if you are scrubbing yourself.

BATHROOM/RESTROOM/TOILET

Make a T handshape with your dominant hand, palm facing outward. Shake your hand side to side.

BED

Make a flat handshape with your dominant hand and touch your palm or back of your hand to the side of your cheek, as if lying down on a pillow.

TIP: This can also be done with both hands.

BRUSH-TEETH

Make a 1 handshape with your dominant hand in front of your mouth, palm facing down. Pull your lips back to expose your teeth and make brushing movements across your teeth as if your fingertip were the toothbrush head.

COOK/PANCAKES

To sign COOK, hold out your nondominant hand in a flat open handshape, palm facing up. With your dominant hand also in a flat handshape, clap each side of the hand down on your nondominant hand, as if cooking something on both sides. Repeat this flipping motion for the full sign. If you make a bigger flipping movement, this becomes the sign for PANCAKES.

HOME

Make a flat O handshape with your dominant hand. Touch the fingertips to the side of your mouth, then move the hand up to the top of your jaw and touch your face again.

TIP: This sign illustrates where you eat and sleep.

HOUSE

With both hands in flat open handshapes, palms facing each other and fingertips touching, move both hands apart and down in one motion.

TIP: This sign shows the roof and walls of a house.

AFTERNOON

With both hands in flat B handshapes, position your nondominant arm in front of the body horizontally. Rest the elbow of your dominant arm on the fingertips of the nondominant hand, with the dominant arm at a 45-degree angle.

ROOM

With both hands held horizontally in flat open handshapes, palms facing inward, bend both wrists back at the same time so both palms face each other.

TIP: Imagine making the four walls of a room.

SHOWER

Make a fist to the side and above your head with your dominant hand. Open your hand into the 5 handshape two times.

TIP: Think of water coming out of the showerhead.

RAIN

With both hands held up in 5 handshapes, palms facing out-ward, bend your wrists and lower your hands so your palms are facing down. Repeat this motion one more time.

SEASON

Make a flat open handshape with your nondominant hand, palm facing to the side, and make an S handshape with your dominant hand, palm facing outward. Place your dominant hand on the palm of your nondominant hand and circle your hand on the palm once.

FALL (SEASON)

Hold up your nondominant arm, hand relaxed. With your dominant hand in a B handshape, brush the side of the nondominant hand two times past your nondominant elbow.

TIP: Think of leaves falling off the "branch" of your nondominant arm.

SPRING (SEASON)

Make a flat C handshape with your nondominant hand, palm facing inward, and make a flat O handshape with your dominant hand, palm facing inward as well. Place the fingertips of the dominant hand in the space inside the flat C hand. Push your dominant hand up through the opening, and as you do, open the hand into a 5 handshape. Repeat this motion two times.

SUMMER

In front of your forehead, make a 1 handshape with your dominant hand, palm facing down. Drag your finger to the other side of your forehead and shift your hand into an X handshape as you move it.

TIP: Think of wiping sweat from your brow.

WINTER

With both hands in W handshapes, palms facing outward, shake your hands side to side.

TIP: This sign is also done with fists, like the sign for COLD (page 92) but without the shivering facial expression.

WEATHER

With both hands in 5 handshapes, palms facing outward, move the hands downward while wiggling them slightly.

TIP: Think of raindrops dripping down a windowpane.

SUN/SUNSHINE

Make a C handshape with your dominant hand, palm facing to the side, and tap the side of the hand to the side of your forehead, next to your eye.

TIP: You can also make this sign by moving the C handshape up toward the sky.

MOON

Make a bent L handshape with your dominant hand. Bend the index finger and touch the thumb to the side of your forehead, then lift the hand up higher and out to the side.

TIP: Most people do an upward glance toward their hand as they make this sign.

COLD (TEMPERATURE)

With both hands in S handshapes held out in front of your body, palms facing each other, shake your hands from side to side as if you were shivering.

TIP: When making this sign, use body language and a facial expression that conveys feeling cold.

HOT (TEMPERATURE)

With your dominant hand in front of your mouth, make a claw handshape, palm facing inward, then quickly rotate the hand outward as you move it away from your mouth.

TIP: Think of putting something very hot in your mouth, then quickly spitting it out.

SNOW

Hold both hands in the air near your head in 5 handshapes. Flutter your fingers as you move your hands down.

TIP: If it is softly falling snow, you can rock the hands slightly from side to side as they move down.

NIGHT/EVENING

Hold up your nondominant arm in front of the body, palm facing down. Make a bent B hand-shape with your dominant hand, palm facing down, and tap that wrist to the back of your nondominant hand.

Signs Involved: Seasons, weather

Instructions: In this lesson, you will test your knowledge of seasons and weather, and learn to distinguish between signs that are similar.

Look carefully at the following nine pictures. Identify the signs in the photos and place the correct term from the word bank below the picture. Then check your responses against the Answer Key (page 243). Remember, some movements look similar to others!

7.

x2

8.

9.

| Fall |
| Hot |
| Rain |
| Snow |
| Spring |
| Summer |
| Sun |
| Weather |
| Winter |

LESSON 5.2: YOUR DAILY SCHEDULE

Signs Involved: Activities, routines

Instructions: In this lesson, you'll create a daily schedule. Choose actions a person might do on a daily basis, using the vocabulary you learned in this chapter. Fill in the blank lines under each time of the day: morning, afternoon, and night. After you have created your schedule, practice signing the information in front of a mirror or video-record yourself to watch how you sign each word.

TIP: When signing a verb, the movement is repeated to represent it in action.

MORNING   **AFTERNOON**   **NIGHT**

Sample

MORNING	AFTERNOON	NIGHT
Brush-Teeth	Exercise	Watch TV
Shower	Dance	Clean Room
Make Bed	Swim	Sleep

My Daily Schedule

MORNING	AFTERNOON	NIGHT
_____	_____	_____
_____	_____	_____
_____	_____	_____

When you are ready to begin signing your schedule, begin with the time of day and then add verbs. Use the following signing prompt to help guide you through this exercise.

Signing Prompt: Time of day (morning, afternoon, night) + Verb

Signing Samples

Morning Brush-Teeth

Afternoon Clean Room

Night Watch TV

LESSON 5.3: SIGNING SENTENCES

Signs Involved: Chapters 1–5 vocabulary

Instructions: In this lesson, you will practice signing sentences to help develop your expressive skills. Here are five sentences for you to practice asking questions and making statements, using the vocabulary you've learned in chapters 1 through 5. Carefully read the English sentence to get a better understanding of how the ASL translation is structured. After you have signed the five sentences, expand your skills by creating your own sentences to practice. Then check your responses against the Answer Key (page 243).

Sign the following sentences.

1. **English Sentence:** In the morning, my sister makes her bed and brushes her teeth.

   ASL Translation: MORNING MY SISTER MAKES BED, BRUSH-TEETH.

2. **English Sentence:** What season do you love?

   ASL Translation: SEASON YOU LOVE (KISS-FIST) WHAT?

3. **English Sentence:** Rachel loves to dance and chat.

   ASL Translation: R-A-C-H-E-L DANCE CHAT LOVES [Please insert space here](KISS-FIST).

4. **English Sentence:** Do you love rain or snow?

   ASL Translation: RAIN SNOW YOU LOVE (KISS-FIST) WHICH?

5. **English Sentence:** My uncle goes hiking.

   ASL Translation: UNCLE MY GO HIKE HE.

CHAPTER 6

TIME & PLACE

In this chapter, you'll not only learn about places and time but also get an understanding of how to identify tenses. As you study this vocabulary, it's especially important to concentrate on the five ASL parameters (handshape, location, movement, palm orientation, and nonmanual markers; see page 8) of each sign. Some signs may differ only by a small change in one or more parameters.

The ASL sentence structure generally puts time in the beginning of the sentence. Establishing the timeline first gives a general idea of when the event or activity took or takes place. The timeline concept in ASL can be challenging at first. Deaf people use different regions around the body to show tenses of past, present, and future.

Example: If a signer signs a time of day, the region from which the signer signs the phrase can change the meaning. For example:

NOW

NIGHT

= TONIGHT

PAST/LAST

NIGHT

= LAST NIGHT

Think of your body as being the center of a timeline. Time signs that are modified to move forward, in front of your body, indicate that they are in the future. Time signs that incorporate a movement toward the back of your body indicate that they are referencing the past.

For example, take the sign for 8 WEEKS. If I add a backward or forward movement to this sign, I am referencing 8 WEEKS AGO or IN 8 WEEKS.

8 WEEKS

ALL-DAY

Hold your nondominant arm in front of your body, palm facing down and touching the elbow of your other arm. With your dominant hand, start with your fingers pointing straight up, then fold your arm down until it lands directly on top of your nondominant arm, both palms facing down.

TIP: Think of the movement of the sun as it travels across the sky.

ALL-NIGHT

Make a flat open handshape with your nondominant hand, palm facing down. Hold this arm in front of your body with your fingertips touching the inner elbow of the dominant arm. With the fingers of your dominant hand pointing down, bring your arm and flat open palm upward until they touch the bottom of your nondominant arm.

TIP: Think of the movement of the sun as it travels around the opposite side of the earth during the night.

DAY

Hold your nondominant arm in front of your body, palm facing down. Make a 1 handshape with your dominant hand and rest the elbow on top of the fingers of your nondominant hand with your index finger pointing straight up. Drop your dominant arm down to the side to land on top of your nondominant arm.

TIP: Instead of 1, you can incorporate other numbers (up to 9) into this sign to show how many days.

EVERYDAY/DAILY

Make an A handshape with your dominant hand and touch the back of your fingers to your jawline, then slide the hand forward two times.

TIP: This sign is similar to the sign for TOMORROW (page 110).

FUTURE

Make a flat handshape with your dominant hand and position your palm at the side of your head, then move the hand forward.

TIP: You can indicate something being further into the future by moving the hand farther forward while squinting your eyes, as if looking at something far away.

MONDAY

Make an M handshape with your dominant hand, palm facing inward, and move it in a small, circular, clockwise motion.

TUESDAY

Make a T handshape with your dominant hand, palm facing inward, and move it in a small, circular, counterclockwise motion two times.

WEDNESDAY

Make a W handshape with your dominant hand, palm facing inward, and move it in a small, circular, counterclockwise motion.

THURSDAY

Fingerspell the letters T-H with your dominant hand. Make a small, circular, clockwise motion with the H.

FRIDAY

Make an F handshape with your dominant hand, palm facing inward, and move it in a small, circular, counterclockwise motion.

SATURDAY

Make an S handshape with your dominant hand, palm facing inward, and move it in a small, circular, counterclockwise motion.

SUNDAY

With both hands in flat open handshapes, palms facing outward at eye level, make small circles with both hands in opposite directions.

HAPPEN/WHEN (STATEMENT)

With both hands held horizontally in 1 handshapes, palms facing up, twist your wrists to rotate the hands so that your palms are facing down. You can also use this to communicate WHEN (as a statement rather than a question).

HOUR/HALF-HOUR

For HOUR, hold up your nondominant hand in a flat handshape, palm facing to the side. With your dominant hand in a 1 handshape, bring your palms together and make a clockwise circle with your dominant hand.

You can use a different number handshape (up to 9) to indicate 2 hours, 7 hours, etc. If you make only a half circle, this is HALF-HOUR.

LAST-WEEK/NEXT-WEEK

For LAST-WEEK, hold the nondominant hand in front of your body, palm facing toward you or up. With the dominant hand in a 1 handshape, palm facing either forward or back, touch the wrist of the dominant hand to the wrist of the palm of the nondominant hand and move across the palm to the fingertips, then continue moving your hand back toward your shoulder.

If you move the dominant hand forward, instead of back toward your shoulder, it becomes the sign for NEXT-WEEK. Instead of the 1, you can sign any number with your dominant hand (up to 9) to say how many weeks ago or how many weeks in the future.

MINUTE

Hold up your nondominant hand in a 1 or flat handshape, palm facing to the side. Make a 1 handshape with your dominant hand and touch the fist to the center of your non-dominant palm. Tick your index finger slightly forward.

TIP: Instead of the 1, you can sign any number with your dominant hand (up to 9) to communicate 5 MINUTES, 8 MINUTES, etc.

MONTH/MONTHLY/RENT (VERB/NOUN)

To sign MONTH, make 1 handshapes with both hands. Position your nondominant hand vertically, palm facing outward, and your dominant hand horizontally, palm facing inward. In a downward motion, drag the dominant index finger down the back of the nondominant index finger one time.

To sign MONTHLY or RENT, repeat the downward motion two or three times.

TIP: Instead of the 1, you can sign any number with your dominant hand (up to 9) as you perform this sign to reflect the number of months. You can also communicate past or future (for example: 7 MONTHS AGO) by making a forward or backward movement with the dominant hand after completing the sign.

TIP: You can turn this into EVERY MORNING by sweeping this sign sideways toward the dominant side of the body.

NEXT-YEAR/LAST-YEAR

For NEXT-YEAR, with both hands in fists stacked in front of the body, dominant hand on top, flick out the dominant index finger while moving the hand forward or up. The nondominant hand remains in place.

LAST-YEAR is signed almost the same way, except the hand and flicking index finger face inward, as if referring to the past.

TIP: You can use your dominant hand to sign numbers (up to 9) as you do LAST-YEAR to show how many years in the past or future.

NOW/TODAY

With both hands in Y handshapes, palms facing up, pull both hands down quickly one time. This is NOW.

If you pull the hands down two times, it becomes the sign for TODAY.

TIME/WHAT-TIME?

For TIME, make an S handshape with your nondominant hand and a 1 handshape with your dominant hand with a slight bend in the finger. Tap your finger on your wrist once, where your watch would be.

To turn this into WHAT-TIME?, simply put a Wh- expression (page 11) on your face while signing TIME.

TOMORROW

Make an open A hand-shape with your dominant hand and touch your cheek with the folded fingers. Arch the hand off the cheek toward the space in front of you, ending in a thumbs-up position.

TONIGHT

This sign is a combination of NOW (page 110) and NIGHT (page 93). For NOW, hold both hands in Y handshapes, palms facing up. Bring the hands down quickly one time, then quickly transition into NIGHT. For NIGHT, hold out your nondominant flat hand with the palm facing down. The dominant hand is in the bent B handshape. Place the wrist of the dominant hand on top of the nondominant hand, with the fingertips over the edge, pointing toward the floor.

TIP: When you sign NIGHT, imagine the bottom hand shows the horizon and the top hand shows the position of the sun in relation to the horizon. In this case, it's under the horizon where you can't see it.

YESTERDAY

Make an A handshape with your dominant hand, palm facing outward. Touch the thumb to the side of your chin, then move the hand back and touch the thumb again near the ear.

WEEK

Hold out your nondominant hand in a flat open handshape, palm facing up. Make a 1 handshape with your dominant hand and touch the palm to the heel of your nondominant palm. Slide the dominant hand across the palm to the fingertips.

TIP: You can also use your dominant hand to show how many weeks (up to 9) by incorporating a number other than 1 into this sign. You can also move the dominant hand back or forward around the hand to communicate past or future, such as 3 WEEKS AGO or IN 5 WEEKS.

WEEKEND

This sign is a combination of WEEK (above) and END. Hold out your nondominant hand in a flat open handshape, palm facing up. Make a 1 handshape with your dominant hand and touch the palm to the heel of the nondominant palm. Slide the dominant hand across the palm to the fingertips. When you reach the fingertips, shift the 1 handshape into a flat handshape and drop it straight downward like the sign for END.

WILL (VERB)

Make a flat open handshape with your dominant hand, palm facing to the side. Hold the hand next to your cheek and move it forward.

TIP: This is the sign used to indicate future tense. Examples: *She will come at 9 p.m.; I will go to the store.*

YEAR

Make fists with both hands, palms facing each other. Rotate the fists around each other, then stack them one on top of the other to conclude.

TIP: Think of your fists as planets rotating around each other.

CHURCH

Make a fist with your nondominant hand, palm facing down, and make a C handshape with your dominant hand, palm facing outward. Tap the thumb of your dominant hand on the back of your nondominant hand two times.

TEMPLE/MOSQUE

Make an S handshape with your nondominant hand, palm facing down, and make a T handshape with your dominant hand, palm facing outward. Tap the base of your dominant hand on the back of your nondominant hand two times. This is TEMPLE.

For MOSQUE, complete the same sign with the dominant hand in an M handshape.

CITY/TOWN

With both hands in open B handshapes, palms facing each other and fingertips together, twist your palms alternately while maintaining contact at the fingertips.

COUNTRY

Hold your nondominant arm up with your hand relaxed near your shoulder. Make a flat hand-shape with your dominant hand and touch the palm to your nondominant elbow, rubbing it in a circular motion two times.

EAST

Hold up your dominant hand in an E hand-shape and slide it to the right.

WEST

Hold your dominant hand up in a W hand-shape and move it to the left.

NORTH

Make an N handshape with your dominant hand, palm facing outward, and slide the hand straight up a few inches.

SOUTH

Make an S handshape with your dominant hand, palm facing outward, and slide the hand straight down a few inches.

LEFT (DIRECTION)

Make an L handshape with your dominant hand, then move it toward your left.

RIGHT (DIRECTION)

Make an R handshape with your dominant hand, then move it toward your right.

FROM

With both hands in 1 handshapes, point your dominant index finger at your nondominant index finger and pull the dominant hand toward your body as the index finger changes into an X handshape.

LIBRARY

Make an L handshape in front of your body with your dominant hand, palm facing outward, and trace two small clockwise circles.

STORE (NOUN)/SELL

For STORE, with both hands in flat O hand-shapes in front of your body, palms facing down, flick your wrists up two times.

To communicate SELL, make one forward movement instead of two.

RESPONSIBLE/DUTY/ OBLIGATION/CHORE

With both hands in flat open handshapes, tap your fingertips to your dominant shoulder two times.

WORK

With both hands in S handshapes, palms facing down, tap the wrist of your dominant hand on the wrist of your nondominant hand two times.

TIP: Think of hammering something.

BUY/SHOP/SHOPPING

To sign BUY, hold out your nondominant hand in a flat handshape, palm facing up. Make a flat O or bent flat handshape with your dominant hand, palm facing down. Place your dominant hand on the palm of your nondominant hand, sliding your dominant hand forward, as if taking money out of your hand and handing it to a cashier.

You can turn the sign for BUY into the sign for SHOP or SHOPPING by repeating the movement.

NOON/MIDNIGHT

Make flat handshapes with both hands and hold your nondominant arm horizontally in front of your body. Place your dominant elbow on top of the fingertips of your nondominant hand so that it is positioned vertically. Point the fingers of your dominant hand upward. This is NOON.

To sign MIDNIGHT, do this sign the same way, except point the fingers of your dominant hand downward, below the arm.

LATE

Lift up the elbow of your dominant arm and let your hand dangle downward in a flat hand-shape with the palm facing inward. Swing your hand outward at the wrist twice, as if swatting at something.

RECENTLY/JUST (ADVERB)

Make an X handshape with your dominant hand, palm facing behind you. Place the side of your bent index finger next to your mouth. Reveal a clenched-teeth expression when making this sign.

TIP: People often tilt their chin toward their dominant shoulder while doing this sign, especially to emphasize that something was very recent.

ALMOST/EASY

With both hands in flat open handshapes, palms facing up, brush the fingertips of your dominant hand along the back of your nondominant fingertips one time.

If you repeat this movement two times, it becomes the sign for EASY.

LESSON 6.1: TIME IS ON YOUR SIDE

Signs Involved: Time and place, vocabulary from chapters 1–6

Instructions: In part 1 of this two-part lesson, you'll look at signs that contain time and tenses (past, present, and future). Your goal is to determine the tense and write it on the lines provided. Check your answers, which are listed on page 245. In part 2, you'll practice signing sentences that include time and places. An English sentence and ASL translation are provided to help you cement your knowledge of ASL sentence structure. Then check your responses against the Answer Key (page 245).

TIP: As you do this lesson, consider the region of the body where the signer begins. This will help you identify the answers.

Part 1: Identify the tense from the pictures provided.

1.

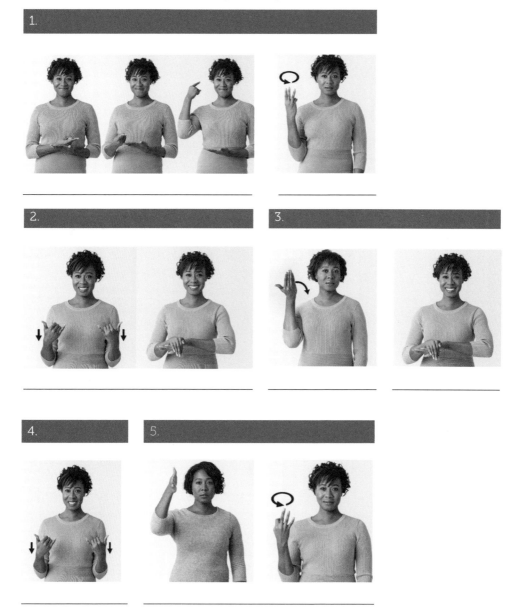

2.

3.

4.

5.

Part 2: In this exercise, practice signing the following sentences. Review the sentences and vocabulary before you begin. If you get stumped, circle the word/words you need to review. Note: (FS) indicates fingerspelling.

1. **English Sentence:** My mom cleaned the house last week on Monday.

ASL Translation: LAST WEEK MONDAY MY MOM HOUSE SHE CLEANED.

2. **English Sentence:** Roger will be at the library all day on Saturday.

ASL Translation: ALL-DAY SATURDAY LIBRARY R-O-G-E-R (FS) THERE WILL.

3. **English Sentence:** My nephew Xavier exercises every day.

ASL Translation: EVERYDAY MY NEPHEW X-A-V-I-E-R (FS) EXERCISES.

4. **English Sentence:** What time is the game on Wednesday?

ASL Translation: WEDNESDAY GAME WHAT-TIME?

5. **English Sentence:** My family will meet you at church next Sunday.

ASL Translation: NEXT WEEK SUNDAY MY FAMILY CHURCH MEET-YOU WILL.

LESSON 6.2: TRANSLATING TIME

Signs Involved (in the correct order): Every, my/mine, family, days of the week, routines, store, walk

Instructions: This lesson will give you practice in translating English sentences into ASL. You'll also identify the tense. After you have identified the tense, think about how the remaining word/words are ordered to match the tense. Before beginning this lesson, it may be helpful to review the information provided in chapter 1 about ASL structure (page 14).

Translate the following sentences into ASL. Follow ASL structure (TIME + TOPIC + COMMENT). Then check your responses against the Answer Key (page 246).

Example:

English Sentence: Every Tuesday, my sister walks to the store.

ASL Translation: EVERY TUESDAY MY SISTER STORE SHE WALKS-TO.

---

1. **English Sentence:** My dad cooked dinner last Thursday.

ASL Translation: _____

---

2. **English Sentence:** On Wednesday, my brother will clean the bathroom.

ASL Translation: _____

---

3. **English Sentence:** When is your grandpa going to work?

ASL Translation: _____

---

4. **English Sentence:** Dakota will celebrate his birthday next month.

ASL Translation: _____

LESSON 6.3: CREATING A FRIEND'S WEEKLY SCHEDULE

Signs Involved: Family and people vocabulary, daily routines, time, place

Instructions: In this lesson, you'll create an imaginary friend's weekly schedule, using vocabulary from earlier in the book. As you look through the vocabulary words you've learned up to this point, think about what your friend might do on a daily basis. Use the words and phrases to add two activities for each day of the week in the blank schedule. After you have created your friend's schedule, practice signing the information in front of a mirror or video-record yourself to watch how you sign each word.

> **TIP:** When signing a verb, the movement is repeated to represent it in action. Also, remember that names can be fingerspelled (FS).

Use the following example to help guide you in designing your friend's daily schedule.

MONDAY	TUESDAY	WEDNESDAY	THURSDAY	FRIDAY	SATURDAY	SUNDAY
Go to temple	Chat with friends	Go to the store	Dance	Play a game	Meet Kevin (FS)	Go shopping
Clean the house	Watch a movie	Clean the bathroom	Cook	Watch TV	Exercise	Go to the library

My Friend's Weekly Schedule

MONDAY	TUESDAY	WEDNESDAY	THURSDAY	FRIDAY	SATURDAY	SUNDAY

LESSON 6.4: CHAPTER 6 VOCABULARY QUIZ

Signs Involved (in the correct order): Time and place

Instructions: This multiple-choice quiz will test your knowledge of the vocabulary you learned in this chapter. Before taking this assessment, feel free to review the vocabulary to familiarize yourself with the signs. Look closely at the pictures and possible answers, as some answers may be similar. Then check your responses against the Answer Key (page 246).

1.

a. Day
b. Everyday/daily
c. Night
d. Afternoon

2.

a. Hour
b. Day
c. Minute
d. Late

3.

a. Saturday
b. Sunday
c. Monday
d. Wednesday

4.

a. Tomorrow
b. Late
c. All-day
d. Now/today

5.

a. Night
b. All-day
c. Work
d. Recently

6.

a. Early
b. What-time?
c. Church
d. Month

7.

a. West
b. East
c. South
d. Future

8.

a. Every day
b. Hour
c. Minute
d. Monday

9.

a. Future
b. Friday
c. Temple
d. From

10.

a. Temple
b. Mosque
c. Church
d. City/town

11.

a. Today/now
b. Tomorrow
c. Thursday
d. Tonight

12.

a. City/town
b. Library
c. Store
d. South

13.

a. Tomorrow
b. Happen
c. Last-week/
   next-week
d. Weekend

14.

a. House
b. Store
c. City/town
d. Temple

15.

a. Minute
b. What-time?
c. Year
d. Hour

CHAPTER 7

FOOD & DRINK

In this chapter, we'll quench your thirst for ASL with signs for different types of foods and a variety of drinks. With the vocabulary in this chapter, you'll be able to create and design your own grocery list. You'll also learn some related vocabulary, and use a compare and contrast model for various types of foods and drinks to express your likes and dislikes and what you want and don't want. Finally, this chapter will provide you with expressive practice to be able to sign to order food at restaurants or fast-food places. Reviewing chapter 4 (page 53) will also help develop your expressive skills around feelings involving food and drinks.

APPLE

Make an X handshape with your dominant hand and touch the back of your finger knuckle to your cheek, twisting your hand forward two times.

BEER

Make a B handshape with your dominant hand, palm facing outward, and hold it next to your dominant cheek. Make small up-and-down or circular motions with your hand.

BREAD

Hold up your nondominant hand in a flat open handshape, palm facing inward. Make a bent B handshape with your dominant hand, and run your fingertips down the back of your nondominant hand two times.

TIP: Think of tracing the slices in a loaf of bread.

BREAKFAST

This sign is a combination of EAT and MORNING. Sign EAT by holding your dominant hand in the flat O handshape, touching your fingertips to your mouth once. Then sign MORNING with both hands in the flat B handshape. Hold your nondominant arm horizontally in front of your body. Hold your dominant hand with palm facing up. Place the fingertips of the nondominant hand on top of the crook of the elbow of the dominant hand. Raise the dominant arm from horizontal to slightly up, just under a 45-degree angle.

CANDY

Make a 1 handshape with your dominant hand. Touch your index finger to your cheek, next to your mouth, and make a double-twisting motion.

TIP: If you smile while making this sign, you can use it to sign DIMPLES.

CHOCOLATE

Hold out your nondominant hand in a fist or flat handshape, palm facing down. Make a C handshape with your dominant hand, touch the back of the thumb to the back of your nondominant wrist, and move your dominant hand in a circular, stirring motion.

TIP: Imagine the circular motion of stirring melted chocolate.

COFFEE

With both hands in S handshapes, palms facing to the side and your dominant hand resting on top of your nondominant hand, move your dominant hand in a counterclockwise circle two times.

TIP: Think of grinding coffee beans.

COOKIE

Hold out your nondominant hand in a 5 handshape, palm facing up. With your dominant hand in a claw handshape, touch the palm of your nondominant hand with your fingertips and twist your dominant hand two times.

TIP: Imagine your dominant hand is a cookie cutter.

CRACKERS

Make an A handshape with your dominant hand and use it to knock the elbow of your nondominant arm two times.

DINNER/SUPPER

This sign is a combination of EAT and NIGHT. First, sign EAT with a flat O handshape brought to your lips once, then quickly sign NIGHT: Hold your nondominant arm in front of your body, horizontally in a flat B handshape. Make a bent B handshape with your dominant hand. Place the wrist of your dominant hand on top of your nondominant hand, with fingertips pointing toward the floor.

DRINK

Make a C handshape in front of your mouth with your dominant hand, palm facing to the side, and pantomime the movement of taking a drink from a cup.

TIP: If you make this sign with an A or Y handshape, you are communicating that the drink is alcoholic.

EAT/FOOD/FEAST

Hold your dominant hand in a flat O hand-shape, and bring it directly to your lips. This is EAT.

If you make a repeated tapping move-ment on the lips, this means FOOD.

If you use both hands in large move-ments, you are communicating FEAST.

EGG

With both hands in U handshapes, stack the fingers of one hand on the fingers of the other, then have them both collapse down-ward in either one or two movements.

TIP: This sign looks somewhat like the action of cracking an egg.

FREEZE/FREEZER/ICE

With both hands in 5 handshapes, palms facing down or outward, stiffen and bend the fingers as you pull your hands closer to your body. This is FREEZE.

If you stiffen and bend the fingers two times, it becomes the sign for FREEZER.

If you sign WATER (page 144) before this sign, making a W handshape with your dominant hand and tapping the side of your index finger to the front of your chin/mouth area two times, it becomes the sign for ICE.

FRENCH-FRIES/TATER-TOTS

For FRENCH-FRIES, make an F handshape with your dominant hand, palm facing outward, and drop your hand slightly forward two times.

If you do this sign with a T handshape, it becomes TATER-TOTS.

FRUIT

Make an F handshape with your dominant hand and touch the pinched index finger and thumb to the side of your cheek, twisting your hand two times.

GLUTEN-FREE

Fingerspell the letters G-F with your dominant hand.

HAMBURGER

Clasp both hands together, one on top of the other, then reverse the orientation so the other hand ends up on top.

TIP: Think of flattening a handful of ground beef into a patty.

HOT-DOG/SAUSAGE

Make fists with both hands, palms facing down, and touch them together end to end. Open your fists slightly, move your hands outward, and close them into fists again.

TIP: Think of connected sausage links that are pinched in sections to separate them.

HUNGRY

Make a C handshape with your dominant hand, palm facing inward. Touch your fingertips to the top of your chest and slide the hand downward, one time, to the stomach.

KETCHUP

Hold up your nondominant fist, palm facing to the side. Make a flat handshape with your dominant hand and hit the top of your nondominant fist with your palm two times.

TIP: Imagine hitting the bottom of a ketchup bottle to move the ketchup to the bottle opening.

LUNCH

This sign is a combination of EAT (page 134) and NOON (page 118). First, sign EAT with a flat O handshape brought to your lips once, then quickly sign NOON: Make flat hand-shapes with both hands, and hold your nondominant arm horizontally in front of the body. Place your dominant elbow on top of the fingertips of your nondominant hand so it is positioned vertically. Point the fingers of your dominant hand upward.

MEAT

Hold out your nondominant hand in a flat handshape, palm facing to the side. With the thumb and index finger of your dominant hand, pinch the space between the thumb and index finger of your nondominant hand.

TIP: Think of holding up a slab of steak.

MILK/DAIRY

Make a loose open S handshape with your dominant hand and squeeze it closed two times.

TIP: Think of the action of milking a cow.

NUTS

Make an A handshape with your dominant hand. Place the tip of your thumb under your two front teeth and pull the hand forward two times.

ONION

Make an X handshape with your dominant hand and touch the index knuckle to the side of your face, next to your eye. Twist the hand forward two times while keeping the knuckle in contact with your face.

TIP: Think of how onions make our eyes water when chopped or sliced.

PEPPER (SPICE)

Make an F handshape with your dominant hand and pantomime the sprinkling of pepper on a plate of food.

PIE

Hold out your nondominant hand in a flat open handshape, palm facing up. Make a flat handshape with your dominant hand, palm facing to the side, and pantomime cutting a slice of pie on the palm of your nondominant hand.

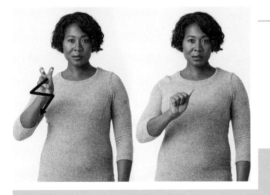

PIZZA

Make a bent V handshape with your dominant hand. Draw the letter Z with your hand, then close the fingers into an A handshape.

TIP: There are many signs for pizza. Defer to your local Deaf community.

POPCORN

Make fists with both hands, palms facing inward, and alternately flick the index fingers upward two or more times.

TIP: Think of popcorn as it pops up out of a hot pot.

SALT

With both hands in V handshapes, rest one V on top of the other V and wiggle the two fingers of the top V handshape.

SANDWICH

Make flat bent handshapes with both hands, palms facing toward the body or down, and stack one on top of the other in front of the mouth. Tap your fingertips to your mouth/chin area slightly two times.

TIP: Think of putting two slices of bread in your mouth.

SODA

Hold out your nondominant hand in a fist, palm facing to the side. With your dominant hand in a 5 handshape, touch the middle finger to the top of your nondominant fist, then immediately touch the entire palm to the fist.

SPAGHETTI

Make I handshapes with both hands, palms facing inward, and point the pinkies toward each other. Move the pinkies away from each other while making curling motions.

TIP: Think of curly spaghetti noodles.

SWEET

Make a flat open handshape with your dominant hand, palm facing inward. Place your fingertips on the tip of your chin and bend your fingers so they slide down and off the chin. The movement can be repeated.

TIP: This is also the sign for the term of endearment SWEETIE.

TEA

Hold out your nondominant hand in a C handshape or fist with the palm facing inward, as if holding a mug. Make an F handshape with your dominant hand and move it in circles above the opposite fist, as if swirling a tea bag around in a teacup.

THIRSTY

Make a 1 handshape with your dominant hand. Touch the tip of your index finger to the top of your throat and trace a straight line down to the bottom of your neck.

TIP: You can communicate the intensity of your thirst with an emphatic facial expression.

VEGETABLE/VEGETARIAN

To sign VEGETABLE, make a V handshape with your dominant hand, palm facing outward. Touch the side of the index finger to the side of your mouth and twist the hand forward a couple of times while maintaining contact.

Add the PERSON sign (page 35) after VEGETABLE to communicate VEGETARIAN. Sign PERSON with both hands in flat open handshapes, palms facing each other but several inches apart. Bring your hands straight down several inches while maintaining the handshapes and palm orientation.

WATER

Make a W handshape with your dominant hand and tap the side of your index finger to the front of your chin/mouth area two times.

WINE

Make a W handshape with your dominant hand. Touch the pinched fingers to your lower cheek and circle your hand two times.

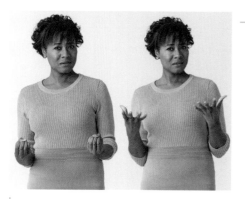

HOW-MANY?/
HOW-MUCH (MONEY)?

To sign HOW-MANY?, with both hands in S handshapes in front of the body, palms facing up, open the hands upward into loose 5 handshapes.

For HOW-MUCH (MONEY)?, sign HOW-MANY? with one hand.

TIP: Show a Wh- expression (page 11) along with this sign.

WANT/DON'T-WANT

For WANT: With both hands in bent 5 handshapes, palms facing up, pull them toward your body while stiffening your fingers into claw handshapes.

To sign DON'T-WANT, turn the palms to face outward while shaking your head.

LIKE/DON'T-LIKE

For LIKE: Make a 5 handshape against your chest with your dominant hand, palm facing inward. Make a pulling motion with your hand, as if pulling a string, and as you pull, bring your thumb and middle fingers together.

For DON'T-LIKE, reverse your wrist so your palm faces outward and flick your middle finger off your thumb, as if you were flicking a piece of lint off your shirt.

HAVE/DON'T-HAVE

For HAVE: With both hands in bent B hand-shapes, bring your fingertips to the sides of your chest, just inside the shoulder blades, in a firm movement.

If you shake your head side to side while making this sign, you are saying DON'T-HAVE.

MUST/NEED/SHOULD/HAVE-TO

Make an X handshape with your dominant hand, palm facing out-ward. Pull your hand downward.

TIP: The intensity of this sign and accompanying facial expression are important to express the urgency of something. *Should* you clean your room, or do you *have to* clean your room?

LESSON 7.1: CHAPTER 7 VOCABULARY QUIZ

Signs Involved (in the correct order): Food and drinks, preferences

Instructions: This multiple-choice quiz will test your knowledge of the vocabulary you learned in this chapter. Before taking this assessment, feel free to review the vocabulary to familiarize yourself with the signs. Look closely at the pictures and possible answers, as some answers may be similar. Then check your responses against the Answer Key (page 246).

1.

a. Popcorn
b. Bread
c. Tea
d. Hungry

2.

a. Apple
b. Candy
c. Beer
d. Thirsty

3.

a. Fruit
b. Apple
c. Candy
d. Sandwich

4.

a. Egg
b. Cookie
c. Coffee
d. Chocolate

5.

a. Drink
b. Hungry
c. Sandwich
d. Thirsty

6.

a. Egg
b. Water
c. Meat
d. Hungry

7.

a. Spaghetti
b. Sandwich
c. Vegetable
d. Crackers

8.

a. Fruit
b. Meat
c. Candy
d. Eat/food/feast

9.

a. Chocolate
b. Eggs
c. Cookie
d. Fruit

10.

a. Egg
b. Spaghetti
c. Popcorn
d. Sweet

11.

a. Sweet
b. Water
c. Thirsty
d. Want

12.

a. Don't-have
b. Want
c. Have
d. Don't-want

13.

a. Coffee
b. Milk
c. Nuts
d. Meat

14.

a. Bread
b. Dinner
c. Eat/food/feast
d. French-fries

15.

a. Apple
b. Spaghetti
c. Coffee
d. Hamburger

LESSON 7.2: TALKING ABOUT FOOD AND QUANTITIES

Signs Involved (in the correct order): Food and drinks, numbers 1–20

Instructions: In this lesson, you will create your own grocery list. As you do, think about the quantity of each item that you would like. Before continuing on to this lesson, this is a great opportunity to review numbers and fingerspelling in chapter 2 (page 17).

When you are signing the grocery list, it's important to sign the vocabulary word first and then the quantity you would like. If the word is fingerspelled, you'll follow the same method. Look at the following example.

Signing Example:

APPLE   **3**

Part 1: Follow the signing prompt. Remember to practice in front of a mirror or video-record yourself.

Signing Sample

ONION   **2**

Onion Quantity 2

Signing Prompt

English Sentence: I need (food + quantity).

ASL Translation: FOOD QUANTITY NEED I.

_____ + _____

1. _____ Quantity: _____

2. _____ Quantity: _____

3. _____ Quantity: _____

4. _____ Quantity: _____

5. _____ Quantity: _____

6. _____ Quantity: _____

7. _____ Quantity: _____

8. _____ Quantity: _____

Part 2: Using the prompt, complete the sentences with the words. Quantities for each sentence are provided for you. Feel free to practice adding your own numbers for additional practice. Practice signing both options (HAVE, DON'T-HAVE).

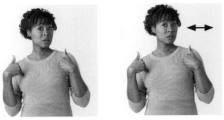

HAVE   **DON'T-HAVE**

Signing Sample: I have 1 hamburger.

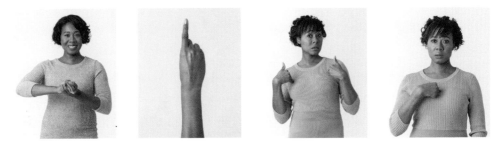

English Sentence: I have/don't have _____ [quantity, food].

ASL Translation: FOOD QUANTITY HAVE/DON'T-HAVE I/ME.

1. Beer   Quantity 3

2. Crackers   Quantity 14

3. Milk   Quantity 2

4. Pies   Quantity 8

5. Eggs   Quantity 24

CULTURAL DISCUSSION: LISTING AND ORDERING

In ASL, to make a list with the information provided, we use a technique called listing and ordering (or ranking). This technique can be used to list and order names, ages, items, family members, and so on.

To list and order, you will use your nondominant hand to show the number of items you are listing. For example, if you have three people in your family, you will create a 3 handshape facing to the side. If you have five items from the grocery store, you will use the 5 handshape facing to the side.

After making the numbered handshape, you'll use your dominant hand to point at your nondominant hand to place the item in the correct order or sequence. Depending on the number of items, your thumb or index finger will be at the top, or first on the list. For example, if you have a 3 handshape, you will point at your thumb first, then go down each finger of the hand for each item you list. If you have a 4 handshape, you will point at your index finger first, then continue going down the other fingers as you list the items.

LESSON 7.3: LISTING AND ORDERING PRACTICE

Signs Involved (in the correct order): Listing and ordering, fingerspelling, numbers, food and drinks

Instructions: Now that you have learned about listing and ordering, let's put this to practice. Sign the following prompts using the listing and ordering technique. Use the examples provided above to help you. Practice this in front of a mirror or video-record yourself.

1. Name your immediate family members, in order from oldest to youngest.

_____

_____

_____

_____

_____

2. Name your top three favorite movies, starting with the best. (Remember, titles of movies are fingerspelled.)

_____

_____

_____

3. Name five of your friends in alphabetical order. (Names are also fingerspelled.)

_____

_____

_____

_____

_____

LESSON 7.4: TELL ME SOMETHING ABOUT YOU

Signs Involved (in the correct order): Food and drinks, fingerspelling, numbers

Instructions: This two-part lesson focuses on creating lists and using the listing and ordering technique to help cement your knowledge of food items. Each of the two exercises will ask you to complete a task. Use the listing and ordering technique for both exercises. Sign the information just as you write it in the outline provided. Before continuing this lesson, feel free to review the listing and ordering technique in lesson 7.3.

> **TIP:** Remember that your nondominant hand is the hand you will use when listing items.

Part 1

Think about your favorite food or dish, using the vocabulary from this chapter. What are the ingredients used to make it? Use the ingredients provided in this chapter. If the ingredient isn't listed, simply fingerspell it! In ASL, many ingredients are fingerspelled because they don't have a sign, including baking soda, cinnamon, flour, and oil. Write out the ingredients in the space provided to help you plan out your signing.

_____

_____

_____

Part 2

Create a grocery list for your family member's upcoming birthday party, using the vocabulary words from this chapter. What items do you need to buy?

_____

_____

_____

CHAPTER 8

ACTIVITIES & EVENTS

Who doesn't love to celebrate life? This chapter focuses on activities and events, so you can talk about and ask questions related to holidays and sporting events. We'll also explore money and relationships.

Throughout this book, you've learned how to translate English sentences to ASL and improved your signing skills. The best way to become comfortable and proficient is to continue practicing these skills. In the lessons provided, you'll have the chance to create your own sentence structures.

Once again, ASL uses tenses when talking about doing activities in the past or the future. Feel free to review the section on tenses (page 14) if you need a refresher before continuing this chapter.

ART

Make a flat handshape with your nondominant hand and hold it in front of your body, palm facing up. With your dominant hand in an I handshape, make a squiggly line down the center of your nondominant hand.

TIP: Think of drawing on a piece of paper with your pinkie finger.

BASEBALL

Hold your hands together in closed fists, one above the other, as if you are holding a baseball bat, and make a couple of small swinging motions.

BASKETBALL

With both hands in 3 handshapes, palms facing each other, rock your hands back and forth.

TIP: There are several signs for BASKETBALL. Always defer to your local Deaf community.

COMPETE/RACE/COMPETITOR/ ATHLETE

To sign COMPETE or RACE: With both hands in A handshapes, thumbs pointed upward, bring your fists together, palms facing each other. Twist your fists alternately, keeping the knuckles together.

To sign COMPETITOR or ATHLETE, add the PERSON sign (page 35) after the COMPETE sign. Sign PERSON with both hands in flat open handshapes, palms facing each other but several inches apart. Bring your hands straight down several inches while maintaining the handshapes and palm orientation.

FOOTBALL

With both hands in 5 handshapes, palms facing each other, bring your hands together and interlock your fingers. Repeat this movement two times.

TIP: Imagine a line of players from two opposing teams crashing together in a tackle.

MAGIC/SPELL

With both hands in flat O hand-shapes, fingertips pointing away from the body, move the hands in half circles before opening both hands quickly into 5 handshapes.

TIP: Imagine sparkles flying out of your fingertips. A mysterious facial expression goes well with this sign.

SOCCER/KICK

To sign SOCCER: Hold out your nondominant hand in a flat open handshape, palm facing to the side or inward. Make a B handshape with your dominant hand, palm facing to the side, and knock it against the bottom of your nondominant hand two times.

Make just one emphasized knocking movement to communicate KICK.

ANNIVERSARY/CELEBRATE

Hold both hands at shoulder height, palms facing each other, and pinch the thumb and index fingers together. Make circular motions with both hands. A celebratory expression goes well with this sign.

TIP: You can communicate specific types of celebrations by identifying the occasion before signing CELEBRATE.

BIRTH

With both hands in flat handshapes, position your nondominant hand in front of your chest or belly, palm facing inward. Touch the palm of your dominant hand to your belly, then move your hand away from your belly until it lands in the palm of your nondominant hand.

TIP: There are other ways to sign BIRTH. Always defer to your local Deaf community.

BIRTHDAY

Make a 5 handshape with your dominant hand, middle finger extended forward and palm facing inward. Place the tip of the middle finger on your chin and then bring it down to touch your chest.

CHRISTMAS

Make a C handshape with your dominant hand, palm facing down. Flip the wrist while moving the hand upward so that the palm faces inward.

TIP: There are multiple variations and signing styles for this sign. Always defer to your local Deaf community.

EASTER

With both hands in E hand-shapes, palms facing each other, twist your wrists so that your palms shift forward two times.

ENGAGED (TO BE MARRIED)

Hold up your nondominant hand in a flat handshape, palm facing down. With your dominant hand in an E handshape, make a circular motion above your nondominant hand before landing it on the ring finger.

FUNERAL

With both hands in V handshapes, palms facing outward, position your dominant hand in front of your nondominant hand. They should not touch. Slide the hands away from your body two times.

TIP: This sign is typically done with a somber facial expression.

HALLOWEEN

With both hands held in front of your face in flat open handshapes, palms facing inward, slide your hands from in front of your face to the sides of your head quickly two times.

TIP: It's like you're playing peekaboo.

HONEYMOON

Make a 5 handshape with your dominant hand, middle finger extended forward. With the tip of this finger, draw a short line down your chin on your dominant side, then another on your nondominant side.

PARADE

Make 5 handshapes with both hands, palms facing down and fingertips extended toward the floor. Position your dominant hand directly in front of your nondominant hand and bend the wrists forward two times in quick movements.

TIP: Think of many legs walking together, as in a parade.

PASSOVER

Make an A handshape with your dominant hand and knock the elbow of your non-dominant arm with it two times.

TIP: The same sign is used for CRACKERS (page 133).

RAMADAN (FASTING)

Make an F handshape with your dominant hand. Place the pinched index finger and thumb on the corner of your mouth, on the nondominant side, and slide it across your lips to end at the opposite corner of your mouth.

ST.-PATRICK'S-DAY

Pinch your dominant thumb and index finger together and touch them to the bicep of your non-dominant arm. Twist the hand once, as if pinching and twisting the skin. Follow with the sign for DAY (page 104): Hold your nondominant arm in front of your body, palm facing inward or down. Make a 1 handshape with your dominant hand and rest your elbow on top of the fingers of your nondominant hand, with your index finger pointing straight up. Drop your dominant arm down to the side to land on top of your nondominant arm.

THANKSGIVING

With both hands in flat open handshapes, palms facing inward, place the fingertips of both hands on or near your chin and move both hands outward, away from your body, at the same time.

TIP: You are basically signing THANK-YOU (page 29) but with both hands instead of one.

VALENTINE'S-DAY

With both hands in 5 handshapes, middle fingers extended forward, touch the tips of your middle fingers to your heart area and draw a heart with both hands. Follow with the sign for DAY (page 104): Hold your nondominant arm in front of your body, palm facing down. Make a 1 handshape with your dominant hand and rest your elbow on top of the fingers of your nondominant hand, with your index finger pointing straight up. Drop your dominant arm down to the side to land on top of your nondominant arm.

VETERANS-DAY

Fingerspell the letters V-E-T with your dominant hand, then follow with the sign for DAY (page 104): Hold your nondominant arm in front of your body, palm facing down. Make a 1 handshape with your dominant hand and rest your elbow on top of the fingers of your nondominant hand, with your index finger pointing straight up. Drop your dominant arm down to the side to land on top of your nondominant arm.

WEDDING

With both hands in flat open handshapes, fingers pointing down and palms facing inward, bring the hands together and end with them clasped.

TIP: Think of two hands joining together in marriage.

BOYFRIEND

This sign is a combination of BOY (page 35) and FRIEND (page 42). First sign BOY in front of the forehead: With your dominant hand, make a pinching movement with all your fingers and move the hand away from the forehead. For FRIEND, with both hands in X handshapes, the palm of your nondominant hand facing up and the palm of your dominant hand facing down, hook your index fingers together briefly and then flip your hands so your dominant hand is now facing up and the nondominant hand is facing down, again hooking your index fingers together briefly.

DENTIST

Make an X handshape with your dominant hand and tap your fingernail to your teeth two times.

TIP: This sign can also be done with an A handshape on the cheek.

FARM/FARMER/RANCH/RANCHER

To sign FARM: Make a 5 handshape with your dominant hand and touch the tip of the thumb to the opposite side of the jaw, sliding the hand to the other side of the jaw while keeping the thumb in contact with your face.

You can add the PERSON sign (page 35) after the sign for FARM to communicate FARMER. Sign PERSON with both hands in flat open handshapes, palms facing each other but several inches apart. Bring your hands straight down several inches while maintaining the handshapes and palm orientation.

You can do the same sign, but change the dominant handshape to an R, to indicate RANCH/RANCHER.

FIANCÉ/FIANCÉE

Hold out your nondominant hand in a flat hand-shape, palm facing down. Make an F handshape with your dominant hand and circle it slightly above the ring finger of your nondominant hand before landing directly on the ring finger.

GIRLFRIEND

This sign is a combination of GIRL (page 36) and FRIEND (page 42). Your dominant hand first signs GIRL with an A handshape, brushing the tip of the thumb down the dominant side of your jawline. For FRIEND, with both hands in X handshapes, the palm of your nondominant hand facing up and the palm of your dominant hand facing down, hook your index fingers together briefly and then flip your hands so your dominant hand is now facing up and the nondominant hand is facing down, again hooking your index fingers together briefly.

MARRIED/DIVORCED

To sign MARRIED, make C handshapes with both hands in front of your body, dominant palm facing down and nondominant palm facing up. Move both hands together until they clasp each other.

One way to sign DIVORCED is by signing MARRIED, then pulling the hands apart and to the sides after clasping them.

PARENTS

This sign is a combination of MOM (page 36) and DAD (page 36). With your dominant hand in the 5 handshape, sign MOM and then DAD in one smooth, quick motion, tapping the chin and then the forehead. This sign is used for one parent or more than one parent, regardless of gender.

PARTNER

With both hands in bent 5 handshapes, palms facing inward, bring the hands together two times in front of your body, interlocking your fingers.

PEOPLE

With both hands in P handshapes in front of the body, palms facing down, move the hands alternately in circles.

AGE/OLD/HOW-OLD?

With your dominant hand, start with a claw handshape or fist in front of your chin, and lower the hand as your handshape changes to an S. For AGE, make two quick downward movements.

For OLD, sign AGE, making one long downward movement.

For HOW-OLD?, make a Wh- expression (page 11) while signing AGE.

CHARGE/COST/FEE/ FINE/PRICE/TAX

Hold out your nondominant hand in a 5 handshape, palm facing inward or to the side. Make an X handshape with your dominant hand and run your index knuckle down the palm of your nondominant hand.

TIP: This sign looks somewhat like holding the trigger of a barcode scanner.

CHEAP

With both hands in flat B handshapes, hold your nondominant hand horizontally, palm facing to the side. With the palm of your dominant hand facing down, swipe the side of the hand across your nondominant palm as it drops.

DOLLAR

Hold out your nondominant hand in a flat handshape, palm facing inward. Clasp the fingers of your nondominant hand with the dominant hand as you slide the dominant hand off the other hand and out to the side.

TIP: Imagine sliding a money clip off a stack of bills.

CENTS

Make a 1 handshape with your dominant hand, palm facing inward, and touch your index finger to the side of your forehead, then move it a few inches away from the forehead without changing the palm orientation.

EXPENSIVE

Hold out your nondominant hand in a flat handshape, palm facing up. With your dominant hand in a flat O handshape, make a gesture that looks like you are picking something up from the palm of the other hand and throwing it off to the side.

TIP: Think of how expensive items can sometimes feel like you are throwing money away.

MONEY

Make a flat handshape with your nondominant hand and a flat B or O handshape with your dominant hand, both palms facing up. Tap the back of your dominant hand to the palm of your nondominant hand two times.

TIP: Think of slapping dollar bills against your palm.

PAY/PAYMENT/PAYMENTS

For PAY or PAYMENT, hold out your nondominant hand in a flat handshape, palm facing up. With your dominant hand in a 1 handshape, touch the fingertip to the middle of your nondominant palm and sweep the finger forward past the fingertips.

You can show the plural concept of PAYMENTS by repeating the PAY sign.

BROKE/BANKRUPT

Make a flat bent handshape with your dominant hand, palm facing down, and make one chopping motion on the neck.

TIP: This sign is sometimes made with both hands for emphasis.

LESSON 8.1: LEARNING CONVERSATIONAL PHRASES

Signs Involved (in the correct order): Activities and events, who, what, when, where, why, fingerspelling

Instructions: In this lesson, you'll practice asking questions and responding using the holidays and events vocabulary. Practice signing each of the following ASL translated questions. After signing the question, write a response in the space provided. Next, practice signing your answers along with the question. When writing responses, try to expand your sentences to more than two or three words, and try to use vocabulary from other units. At the end of the lesson, you will have the chance to write your own English question, ASL translation, and response.

TIP: When you are signing two or more signs for comparing, contrasting, or separation of information, use the shoulder shift method. Shoulder shifting is used to differentiate information and details within a sentence. To show this, move your head and shoulders in different directions (side to side) to reference a piece of new information being compared, contrasted, or separated. Be careful not to exaggerate the movement of the shoulder and head movement. A slight movement can easily change a detail in the information presented.

TIP: In ASL, months are fingerspelled, but you can abbreviate the months that can be shortened, such as January = Jan., February = Feb., November = Nov.

1. **English Sentence:** When is your birthday?

ASL Translation: BIRTHDAY YOURS WHEN?

Response: _____

2. **English Sentence:** What month is your anniversary?

ASL Translation: ANNIVERSARY MONTH YOURS WHAT?

Response: _____

3. **English Sentence:** What is your father's/mother's favorite sport?

ASL Translation: YOUR FATHER/MOTHER FAVORITE SPORT WHAT?

Response: _____

4. **English Sentence:** Is your uncle/aunt married or divorced?

ASL Translation: YOUR UNCLE/AUNT MARRIED DIVORCED WHICH?

Response: _____

5. **English Sentence:** How much does it cost to go to the basketball game?

ASL Translation: BASKETBALL GAME TO-GO-TO COST HOW MUCH?

Response: _____

Independent Practice: Practice writing your own question. Include an English sentence, ASL translation, and response, using the vocabulary from this chapter. Review the instructions for translating an English sentence to ASL in chapter 1 (page 14).

6. **English Sentence:** _____

ASL Translation: _____

Response: _____

LESSON 8.2: INTENTIONAL CONVERSATIONS ABOUT YOU AND YOUR FAMILY

Signs Involved (in the correct order): Holidays and events, family, likes, dislikes, numbers

Instructions: This lesson has two parts. In the first part, you'll fill in the blanks using the vocabulary in this chapter. After filling in the blanks, you'll practice signing the sentences. Practice in front of a mirror or video-record yourself for best results.

In part 2, you'll create sentences on your own using the vocabulary words you have learned so far. Be sure to use vocabulary from other chapters to help you complete each sentence. Before signing the sentences, review the vocabulary signs. Then check your responses against the Answer Key (page 246).

Part 1: Fill in the blanks with the vocabulary in this chapter to complete the sentences. Then practice signing the sentences.

1. My brother's/sister's anniversary month is _____.

2. My _____ does not like to celebrate _____.

3. My _____ spent $400 to see a baseball game.
   It was expensive/cheap.

4. My parents got married when they were _____ (age).

Part 2: Using the vocabulary from this chapter and throughout the book, create your own sentences. Try to use one or more vocabulary words from each chapter you have completed.

1. _____

2. _____

3. _____

4. _____

LESSON 8.3: CHAPTER 8 VOCABULARY QUIZ

Signs Involved (in the correct order): Holidays and events

Instructions: This multiple-choice quiz will test your knowledge of the vocabulary you learned in this chapter. Before taking this assessment, feel free to review the vocabulary to familiarize yourself with the signs. Look closely at the pictures and possible answers, as some answers may be similar. Then check your responses against the Answer Key (page 248).

1.

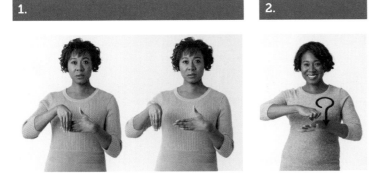

a. Dollar
b. Cents
c. Events
d. Money

2.

a. Married
b. Engaged
c. Fiancé/fiancée
d. Divorced

3.

a. Dentist
b. Farm/farmer/
   ranch/rancher
c. Honeymoon
d. Aunt

4.

a. Parade
b. Funeral
c. People
d. Parents

5.

a. Valentine's-Day
b. Honeymoon
c. St.-Patrick's-Day
d. Wedding

6.

a. Money
b. Cents
c. Broke/bankrupt
d. Cost

7.

a. Parade
b. People
c. Married
d. Divorced

8.

a. Halloween
b. Celebrate
c. Event
d. Thanksgiving

9.

a. Football
b. Baseball
c. Fiancé/fiancée
d. Girlfriend

10.

a. Funeral
b. Passover
c. Buy
d. Baseball

11.

a. Anniversary
b. Age
c. Ramadan
d. Easter

12.

a. Dentist
b. Farm
c. Engaged
d. Art

13.

a. Cents
b. Dollar
c. Broke/bankrupt
d. Cost/charge

14.

a. Magic
b. Art
c. Baseball
d. Football

15.

a. Funeral
b. Parade
c. Magic
d. Birthday

CHAPTER 9

TRAVEL

Pack your bags! In this chapter, you'll learn how to sign about traveling and various transportation methods. As you study this chapter, you'll want to look closely at the similarities and differences in signs.

Before beginning this chapter, reflect on the vocabulary words you have learned so far. You will be asked to demonstrate your knowledge of signs taught throughout this chapter and incorporate them with signs from previous chapters. In fact, the lessons in this chapter will allow you to practice your expressive skills by combining all the vocabulary words you have learned throughout this book. One lesson focuses on planning an upcoming family vacation or short trip. This is a great time to consider challenging yourself in expanding on your expression to more than just a sentence or two!

AIRPLANE/FLY

For AIRPLANE, make an open handshape with your dominant hand, palm facing outward, and fold down your middle and ring fingers, keeping the other three fingers open. Slide the hand forward in two quick movements.

To sign the verb FLY, make the same handshape with your dominant hand as you did for AIRPLANE, but instead of two quick forward movements, make one long forward movement.

BACK-AND-FORTH

Make an open A handshape with your dominant hand, palm facing to the side and thumb pointing upward, then move your hand in, out, then back in.

BICYCLE

Make fists with both hands and hold them in front of your body, palms facing down, as if holding the handlebars of a bicycle. Now rotate your fists in alternating circles, as if pedaling a bicycle.

BOAT

With both hands cupped, palms facing up and positioned side by side so your hands resemble a boat, bounce your hands up and down a couple of times.

TIP: Think of your hands as a boat crashing through waves.

BREAK-DOWN (ENGINE)

With both hands in claw handshapes, palms facing each other, interlock your fingers and drop your hands downward as your fingers break away from each other.

TIP: Think of your hands as interlocked gears breaking apart.

CAR/DRIVE

To sign CAR, hold out both hands in fists, as if they were grasping a steering wheel, and move them alternately up and down as if you were swerving from side to side.

To sign the verb DRIVE, move the fists in a smooth forward motion rather than a swerving motion.

CLOSE-BY

Make an F handshape with your dominant hand, palm facing inward. Brush the tip of your pinched index finger and thumb off the tip of your nose in a downward direction. As you do so, hold your mouth in a tight O shape.

COMMUTE

Make a thumbs-up handshape with your dominant hand in front of your body and move it side to side several times.

TIP: Think of repeatedly traveling the path between two places.

FIX/REPAIR

With both hands in flat O handshapes, brush the tops of the fingertips of both hands past each other two times.

FOLLOW/CHASE

With both hands in thumbs-up handshapes, put one fist in front of the other, then move both hands forward. This is FOLLOW.

If you move the back fist in a circular movement throughout, this sign becomes CHASE.

GASOLINE

Hold out your nondominant hand in a fist, palm facing to the side, and tap the tip of your dominant thumb into the tight space made by the closed fist.

TIP: Think of inserting a gas nozzle into a vehicle.

GET-IN

Make a C handshape with your nondominant hand, palm facing to the side, and make a bent V handshape with your dominant hand. Imagine that both fingers are legs and your C hand is a vehicle. "Seat" the fingers of your dominant hand by hooking them on to the thumb of your nondominant hand.

GET-OUT

This is signed the same way as GET-IN, except you unhook the fingers of your dominant hand from your nondominant thumb to mimic a person getting out of a vehicle.

MOTORCYCLE/SNOWMOBILE

For MOTORCYCLE, with both hands in fists and held out in front of the body as if holding handlebars, twist the wrist of your dominant hand back and forward two times as if revving a motorcycle.

For SNOWMOBILE, hold both hands up in the air near your head in 5 handshapes. Flutter your fingers as you move your hands down, then sign MOTORCYCLE.

x3

RENTAL

Make 1 handshapes with both hands. Your nondominant hand is positioned vertically, palm facing outward. Your dominant hand is positioned horizontally, palm facing inward. In a downward movement, drag the dominant hand down the nondominant hand three times. This is the same sign as MONTH, but the repetition of the movement communicates RENTAL. Use this sign no matter the length of the time of the rental.

RIDE-IN/RIDE-ON

Make a C handshape with your nondominant hand, palm facing to the side, and make a bent 2 handshape with your dominant hand, palm facing down. Hook the bent 2 fingers on the thumb of the C hand. Pull the C hand forward, moving the bent 2 hand with it.

TIP: Imagine a person sitting in a vehicle as it moves forward.

SUBWAY

Make a flat or B handshape with your nondominant hand, palm facing down, and make a Y handshape with your dominant hand, palm facing outward. Place your dominant hand underneath your nondominant hand. Move your dominant hand forward and backward two times.

TAXI

Fingerspell the letters T-A-X-I with your dominant hand.

TICKET

Make a flat open handshape with your nondominant hand, palm facing inward, and make a bent V handshape with your dominant hand, palm facing to the side. Straddle the two bent fingers around the bottom of your nondominant hand, repeating the movement two times.

TIP: Imagine a ticket taker punching a hole in a ticket.

TRAFFIC

Make 5 handshapes with both hands, palms facing down and your dominant hand positioned in front of your nondominant hand. Bring the hands forward in two quick stop-and-go motions.

TIP: Imagine looking down from a tall building at cars backed up in rows.

TRAIN (NOUN)

With both hands in U handshapes, palms facing down, touch the fingers of your dominant hand to the top of the fingers of your nondominant hand and rub the dominant fingers back and forth.

TRAVEL

Make a bent V handshape with your dominant hand, palm facing down, and move the hand in a large forward-arching sweep.

AFRICA

With your dominant hand, make a flat O handshape in front of your body, palm facing outward. Trace the shape of Africa by opening your hand into a wide C handshape and closing your hand back into a flat O handshape as you reach the tip of the continent. This entire sign is done in a smooth, fluid motion.

AMERICA/UNITED-STATES

With both hands in 5 handshapes, fingers straight and interlaced and palms facing inward, move your interlaced hands in a counterclockwise circle. This is AMERICA.

UNITED-STATES is fingerspelled U-S.

TIP: You can combine UNITED-STATES and AMERICA to say UNITED STATES OF AMERICA.

AREA/FIELD/GROUND

Make a 5 handshape with your dominant hand, palm facing down, and move it in a circular, counterclockwise motion two times. This sign can be used for AREA; FIELD; GROUND, as in playground; or other bodies of ground space.

ASIA

Make an A handshape with your dominant hand, palm facing outward. Move it downward and out to the side in a circular motion, but as your hand starts the upward motion of the circle, make a 5 handshape and end above where your A hand started.

AUSTRALIA

With both hands in 8 handshapes, palms facing down, bring your hands up and forward in an upward arch, ending the arch by opening your hands into 5 handshapes.

BEACH

Hold up your nondominant hand in a flat handshape, palm facing down. Make a flat O handshape with your dominant hand and rest it on top of your nondominant hand. The fingers of your dominant hand should be pointing toward you. Make a 5 handshape with your dominant hand as you slide it closer to your body, then slide it back into the O handshape again. Repeat two times.

TIP: This sign looks like waves crashing on a shore.

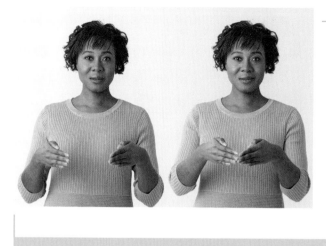

CORNER

With both hands in flat B handshapes and positioned horizontally, bring the fingertips of both hands together to form a right angle, or corner, with your hands.

TIP: You're showing two lines meeting together at a corner.

EARTH

Make an S handshape with your nondominant hand and make an open 8 handshape with your dominant hand. Place the tips of your dominant middle finger and thumb on the back of your nondominant hand and wiggle the hand forward and back.

EUROPE

Make an E handshape with your dominant hand, palm facing to the side, and draw a circle with it near the side of your forehead.

FAR

With both hands held together in front of the body in A handshapes, palms facing each other, move the dominant fist forward and slightly upward while keeping the nondominant fist in place.

TIP: Think of one hand being far ahead of the other one.

HOTEL

Make a 1 handshape with your nondominant hand, palm facing to the side in a vertical position. Make an H handshape with your dominant hand, palm facing inward. Place the dominant hand on the tip of the nondominant index finger and tap the air toward your body with the dominant fingers.

ARRIVE

Make flat open handshapes with both hands, palms facing up. Hold out both hands, with your dominant hand starting above your nondominant hand, then move your dominant hand forward and downward till it lands on the nondominant palm.

TIP: Think of your dominant hand arriving at or landing on your nondominant hand.

NORTH-AMERICA

This sign is a combination of NORTH (page 115) and AMERICA (page 194). First, use your dominant hand to sign NORTH with an N handshape, palm facing outward, by sliding the hand straight up a few inches. Then sign AMERICA with both hands in 5 handshapes, fingers straight and interlaced and palms facing inward. Move your interlaced hands in a counterclockwise circle.

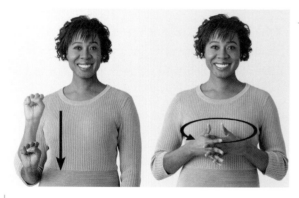

SOUTH-AMERICA

This sign is a combination of SOUTH (page 115) and AMERICA (page 194). First, use your dominant hand to sign SOUTH with an S handshape, palm facing outward, by sliding the hand straight down a few inches. Then sign AMERICA with both hands in 5 handshapes, fingers straight and interlaced and palms facing inward. Move your interlaced hands in a counterclockwise circle.

STATE (NOUN)

Hold up your nondominant hand in a flat open handshape, palm facing at an angle away from the body. Make an S handshape with your dominant hand and knock the side of the fist at the top of your nondominant hand and again at the bottom.

UNIVERSE/WORLD

With both hands in U handshapes, rotate the hands around each other one time and then rest one on top of the other. This is UNIVERSE.

WORLD is signed the same way as UNIVERSE; just use W handshapes for WORLD.

OUTSIDE

Hold up your dominant hand in a 5 handshape, palm facing inward, then pull the hand away from your body a couple of times as the fingers come together into a flat O handshape.

FINISHED/ALL-DONE

With both hands in front of your body in 5 handshapes, palms facing inward, shake both hands briskly, as if trying to air-dry wet hands.

LONG/HOW-LONG?

To sign LONG, hold up your nondominant arm, palm facing down. Make a 1 handshape with your dominant hand and draw a line with your index finger up the back of your nondominant arm, starting near your wrist and ending near your shoulder.

To ask HOW-LONG?, show a Wh- expression (page 11) on your face while signing LONG.

NOT-YET

Lift up the elbow of your dominant arm and let your hand dangle downward in a flat hand-shape with the palm facing inward. Swing your hand outward at the wrist, as if swatting at something. While doing this sign, open your mouth and stick your tongue out slightly.

TIP: The mouth movement may feel silly, but it is an important part of the sign. If you don't make the mouth movement, you will be signing LATE rather than NOT-YET.

PAST/LONG-TIME-AGO

To sign PAST, make a flat open handshape with your dominant hand positioned above your dominant shoulder, palm facing behind you. Wave the hand backward a couple of times.

To show LONG-TIME-AGO, make bigger and more prolonged backward gestures with an emphatic facial expression.

FINALLY/AT-LAST

Touch both index fingertips to your chin, palms facing inward, then reverse the palms outward while moving your hands away from the body and out to the sides of your face.

TIP: This sign has a nonmanual marker that accompanies it: Quietly say "PAH!" as you move your fingers outward.

SOMETIMES/ONCE-IN-A-WHILE

To sign SOMETIMES, hold out your nondominant hand in a flat handshape, palm facing up or to the side. Make a 1 handshape with your dominant hand and touch the side of your index fingertip to your nondominant palm in a circular motion a couple of times.

To communicate something happening only ONCE-IN-A-WHILE, make a bigger circular motion.

SOON

Make an F handshape with your dominant hand, palm facing inward and held horizontally. Place the pinched fingers on your chin and move them downward a couple of times. As you do this sign, move your mouth into a pursed O shape.

LESSON 9.1: ASKING QUESTIONS ABOUT TRANSPORTATION AND TRAVELING

Signs Involved (in the correct order): Transportation and traveling, time and place, fingerspelling, numbers, yes and no

Instructions: In this lesson, you'll practice asking questions and responding using your newly acquired vocabulary of transportation and traveling words. Here you'll see some English sentences and their ASL translations. Practice signing each ASL-translated question. Sign in front of a mirror or video-record yourself to ensure you are signing accurately. Then check your responses against the Answer Key (page 248).

1. **English Sentence:** What time is the flight (sign = AIRPLANE)?

ASL Translation: AIRPLANE (FLIGHT) YOUR LEAVE WHEN?

2. **English Sentence:** Do you have your ticket?

ASL Translation: TICKET YOURS YOU HAVE?

3. **English Sentence:** Are you from North America or South America?

ASL Translation: NORTH-AMERICA SOUTH-AMERICA YOU FROM WHICH?

4. **English Sentence:** My sister/brother is from Asia.

ASL Translation: SISTER/BROTHER MINE FROM ASIA.

5. **English Sentence:** Do you take the taxi to the train station?

ASL Translation: YOU RIDE-IN TAXI GO-TO TRAIN AREA?

6. **English Sentence:** How long is the subway ride to the beach?

ASL Translation: SUBWAY RIDE-IN BEACH HOW-LONG?

7. **English Sentence:** I visited Europe and Australia last year.

ASL Translation: LAST-YEAR VISIT EUROPE AUSTRALIA FINISHED I.

8. **English Sentence:** Please put gas in the rental car soon.

ASL Translation: SOON RENTAL-CAR PUT GAS PLEASE.

LESSON 9.2: PLAN YOUR DAILY ROUTINE FOR A VACATION OR BUSINESS TRIP

Signs Involved (in the correct order): Traveling and transportation, daily routines, time and place, food and drink

Instructions: In this lesson, you'll be planning a vacation itinerary. Review and use the vocabulary from this chapter, as well as chapters 5 (Daily Routines), 6 (Time & Place), and 7 (Food & Drink) to make specific plans for your trip. When you're ready to sign, sign the information in the order presented in the outline. I recommend video-recording yourself signing this information and rewatching it. This will help with you being able to sign all the information at your own pace to see how it all looks when it comes together. Any words you don't know can be fingerspelled, so go ahead and get creative with your responses—this is your trip, after all! Check your responses against the Answer Key (page 250).

Monday

- Flight at _____ (number) a.m.
- Arrive in _____ (country or continent).
- Taxi to _____ (city/town).
- Sleep in the hotel.

Tuesday

- Wake up at _____ a.m.
- Eat breakfast.
- Ride the subway to _____ (attraction).
- Take a bicycle back to the hotel.

Wednesday

- Wake up at _____ a.m.
- Rent a car and visit the city.
- Go to the cafe to eat lunch.
- _____ (verb) at the beach.

Thursday

- Wake up at _____ a.m.
- Shower at the hotel.

- Take a _____ (transportation) to the airport.
- Arrive back in North America.

Friday

- Clean my motorcycle.
- Ride close by town.
- Exercise in the _____ (time of day).

Saturday

- Take a taxi to the library
- Drink coffee outside.
- Eat dinner at 7 p.m.

Sunday

- Take a train to church.
- Eat lunch with friends from Australia
- Hike at the beach in the afternoon.

Planning a trip takes time, and so does learning to sign! Feel free to complete this lesson over a few sessions—there's no need to do this all at once. Maybe answer and sign a few entries each day, and when you've got your trip all mapped out, see if you can sign the whole adventure.

LESSON 9.3: CHAPTER 9 VOCABULARY QUIZ

Signs Involved (in the correct order): Transportation and traveling

Instructions: This multiple-choice quiz will test your knowledge of the vocabulary you learned in this chapter. Before taking this assessment, feel free to review the vocabulary to familiarize yourself with the signs. Look closely at the pictures and possible answers, as some answers may be similar. Then check your responses against the Answer Key (page 257).

1.

a. Get-in
b. Follow/chase
c. Australia
d. Back-and-forth

2.

a. Beach
b. Asia
c. Gasoline
d. Corner

3.

a. Airplane
b. Taxi
c. Boat
d. Car/drive

4.

a. Ride-in
b. Get-in
c. Ticket
d. Commute

5.

a. Gasoline
b. Here
c. State
d. Ticket

6.

a. Australia
b. Africa
c. Asia
d. North-America

7.

a. Asia
b. Area
c. Beach
d. Universe/world

8.

a. State
b. Asia
c. Here
d. North-America

9.

a. Africa
b. Australia
c. Church
d. Universe/world

10.

a. Beach
b. Area
c. Fix
d. Traffic

11.

a. Area
b. Here
c. Corner
d. Fix

12.

a. Follow/chase
b. Here
c. Get-in
d. Ride-in

13.

a. House
b. State
c. Earth
d. Country

14.

a. Asia
b. Europe
c. Earth
d. State

15.

a. Subway
b. Boat
c. Universe
d. Break-down

16.

a. Back-and-forth
b. Commute
c. Fix
d. Get-in

17.

a. Rental
b. Boat
c. Fix
d. Close-by

18.

a. Close-by
b. Traffic
c. Country
d. Taxi

19.

a. Australia
b. North-America
c. Earth
d. Africa

20.

a. Earth
b. Universe/world
c. Country
d. Europe

21.

a. Gasoline
b. Far
c. From
d. Country

22.

a. Drive
b. Ride-in
c. Subway
d. Far

23.

a. Left
b. Right
c. Far
d. From

24.

a. Hotel
b. Commute
c. Break-down
d. Universe/world

25.

a. City/town
b. Farm
c. Asia
d. Europe

HEALTH, SAFETY & COLORS

You did it! You've made it to the final chapter. Chapter 10 will focus on some more practical concepts, including health, safety, and colors. We'll kick things off, though, with a cultural discussion about the differences between Deaf versus deaf. By the end of this chapter, you'll be equipped to express various health situations, identify colors, and learn more about how to continue your ASL education. Before completing the lessons at the end of this chapter, review the family signs in chapter 3 (page 27)—doing so will be helpful.

When signing about health and colors, it's important to remember that many signs look similar. Because of this, it's worth circling back to chapter 1 (page 1) to review the parameters of ASL: handshape, location, movement, palm orientation, and nonmanual markers.

CULTURAL DISCUSSION:
BIG-D DEAF VS LITTLE-D DEAF

You may have seen two different spellings for Deaf: one with an uppercase D and another with a lowercase d. What's the difference?

Deaf with an uppercase D refers to people who relate to and identify as a member of the Deaf community, through language and culture. Oftentimes people who identify as Deaf with the uppercase D are either born into a Deaf family, are active members in the Deaf community, or have family members who are Deaf.

There are more ways a Deaf person may join the Deaf community. A person who was born Deaf to hearing parents may at some point decide to be part of the Deaf community and its culture. In addition, a person who becomes Deaf later in life, known as late-deafened, may also choose to become part of the Deaf community.

People who identify as deaf with a lowercase d are often those who do not use sign language or identify with Deaf culture. In short, deaf represents the physical condition of hearing loss. A person identifying as deaf likely does not use sign language and prefers to use only speech. For example, a deaf person may have been born deaf, but grew up with hearing parents who primarily exposed them to hearing culture rather than Deaf culture.

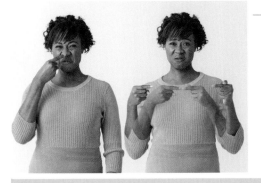

ALLERGY/ALLERGIES

This sign has two parts. First, touch your nose with the index finger of your dominant hand. Second, touch both of your index fingers together, then move them away from each other quickly.

TIP: The movement of this sign is like two magnets pushing away from each other.

AMBULANCE

With both hands in bent 5 handshapes, palms facing outward and hands above the head, twist your wrists back and forth.

APPOINTMENT/ RESERVATION

With both hands in
A handshapes, hold your nondominant hand out in front
of your body at a 45-degree
angle, palm facing down.
Hold your dominant hand just
above your nondominant hand and circle around it in a clockwise direction to form a half circle in the air. Then drop your dominant hand down
on top of your nondominant wrist.

BAND-AID

Make a fist with your nondominant hand, palm
facing down. With your dominant hand in an
H handshape, pull the fingertips across the back of
your nondominant hand.

TIP: This sign looks like your fingers are tracing a Band-Aid
on the back of your wrist.

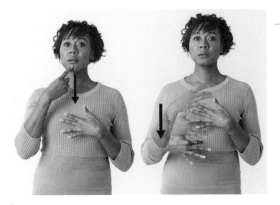

BLOOD

This sign has two parts. First, sign RED (page 226) by stroking the index finger of your dominant hand down your chin. Second, with both hands in 5 handshapes positioned horizontally, dominant hand in front of the nondominant hand and palms facing inward, wiggle the fingers of your dominant hand in a downward motion.

COLD (ILLNESS)

With your dominant hand, make a double-pinching downward movement from the tip of your nose with your thumb and index finger.

TIP: Think of wiping your nose with a tissue.

COUGH

Make a fist with your dominant hand and knock your fist against your upper chest two or more times.

TIP: Think of trying to clear your lungs of an obstruction.

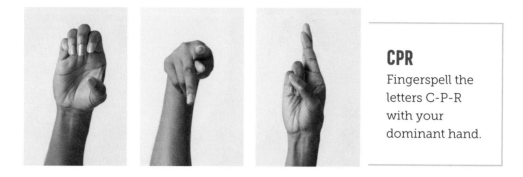

CPR

Fingerspell the letters C-P-R with your dominant hand.

DIZZY

Make a claw handshape and hold it by the side of your forehead, palm facing inward, making a circular motion with your hand.

TIP: Imagine things jumbling around in your skull. Make a confused expression along with this sign.

DOCTOR

Hold out your nondominant hand in a flat handshape, palm facing up. Make a flat bent handshape with your dominant hand and touch the tips of your fingers to your nondominant wrist two times.

EMERGENCY

Make an E handshape with your dominant hand, palm facing outward, and shake your hand side to side a few times.

TIP: Think of waving to get someone's attention due to an urgent situation.

HEART

Make a 5 handshape with your dominant hand, middle finger extended forward and palm facing inward. Tap the middle finger to the heart area of your chest two times.

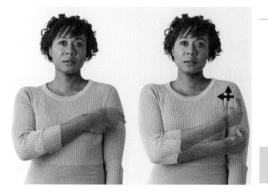

HOSPITAL

Make an H handshape with your dominant hand and draw a plus sign on the side of your nondominant arm.

TIP: Think of the American Red Cross.

HURT/PAIN

With both hands in 1 handshapes, point the index fingers at each other and twist the hands in the opposite directions.

TIP: This is a locational sign, so you can also make this sign in front of the area of the body that is hurting—for example, near the head to indicate a headache, or near the mouth to indicate a toothache.

INFECTION/INSURANCE

For INFECTION, hold your dominant hand up near your shoulder in an I handshape, palm facing outward, and shake it side to side. People often scrunch up their face in disgust while doing this sign.

Without a facial expression, this sign is also INSURANCE.

MEDICINE

Hold out your nondominant hand in an open handshape, palm facing up. With your dominant hand in a 5 handshape, palm facing down, extend the middle finger and touch it to the center of your nondominant palm, then wiggle your dominant hand slightly.

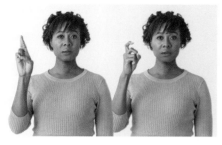

RX (PRESCRIPTION)

Sign the letters R-X quickly with your dominant hand.

SICK

With both hands in 5 handshapes, middle fingers extended forward, place the tip of your dominant middle finger on the side of your forehead and the tip of your nondominant middle finger on the side of your stomach.

TIP: Show an expression of not feeling well with this sign.

SNEEZE

Make a 1 handshape with your dominant hand, palm facing down, and touch the side of the index finger to the space under your nose while dropping your head forward forcefully.

TIP: Think of the body movement that often accompanies a powerful sneeze.

STROKE (MEDICAL)

Make a flat open handshape with your dominant hand, palm facing to the side. Starting at the forehead, draw a zigzagging line in the space in front of the body.

TIP: There are other ways to sign this word. Defer to your local Deaf community.

TAKE-PILL

Make a fist with your dominant hand, extend the thumb and index fingers, and press the fingernail of your index finger to the tip of the thumb. Bring your hand toward your mouth and flick your index finger in the direction of your slightly open mouth, as if popping a pill. If you flick the finger two times, it becomes PILL (noun).

THROW-UP/VOMIT

Make 5 handshapes with both hands, palms facing to the sides, and position your dominant hand close to your mouth with your nondominant hand right in front of it. Move both hands forcefully forward and downward.

TIP: Make sure your face matches what the sign is communicating.

NURSE

Hold out your nondominant hand in a flat open handshape, palm facing up. Make a U handshape with your dominant hand and tap the two fingers to the wrist of your nondominant hand two times.

TIP: Think of taking someone's pulse.

BONE

With both hands in bent V handshapes, palms facing inward, cross your arms at the wrists and tap the wrists together two times.

BREAK (FRACTURE)

With both hands together in S handshapes in front of your body, palms facing down, twist your wrists in opposite directions as if you were snapping a stick in half.

x2

BRAIN

Make an X handshape with your dominant hand and tap the index fingertip to the side of your forehead two times.

TIP: It looks as if you are tapping at your brain inside your skull.

BREATH/BREATHE

With both hands in 5 handshapes, palms resting against your chest and stomach, move the hands away from the body a few inches and then bring them back to the chest and stomach.

TIP: Imagine the lungs expanding and contracting. You can also show that someone is short of breath by repeating the movement quickly several times while showing a panting expression.

FEET

Make a 1 handshape with your dominant hand and make downward pointing motions in the direction of each foot.

TIP: You do not need to lean down to get closer to your feet for this sign.

GROW-UP

Make a flat open handshape with your dominant hand, palm facing down. Start with your hand at waist height and raise it upward.

TIP: Think of your hand being on top of a child's head as they grow taller and taller.

HAIR

Pinch and pull on your hair with your dominant hand.

TEMPERATURE

Hold up your nondominant hand in a
1 handshape, palm facing outward. Make a
1 handshape with your dominant hand as
well, palm facing inward, and slide the index
finger up and down the back of the nondominant index finger.

TIP: Think of how mercury rises and falls in
a thermometer.

SKIN

Using your thumb and your bent index finger,
pinch your cheek.

STAND

Hold out your nondominant hand in a flat
handshape, palm facing up. With your dominant hand in a V handshape, touch the two
fingertips to the center of the nondominant
palm, like legs standing on a flat surface.

TIP: If you move both hands in a forward circular
movement while making this sign, you are communicating standing for a long period of time.

STRONG

Make fists with both hands, palms facing inward, near the dominant shoulder. Pull both fists forward forcefully, away from the body, in the same direction.

TOOTH/TEETH/GLASS (MATERIAL)

To sign TOOTH or GLASS, make an X hand-shape with your dominant hand and tap your index fingertip to your teeth.

To sign TEETH, slide your fingertip across several teeth rather than tapping just a few.

FAVORITE/PREFER

Make a 5 handshape with your dominant hand and extend the middle finger forward. Tap the tip of your middle finger to your chin two times.

COLOR/COLORFUL

To sign COLOR, make a 5 handshape with your dominant hand, palm facing inward, then touch your fingertips to your chin and wiggle your fingers.

If you make this sign with both hands, touching the chin alternately, it becomes the sign for COLORFUL.

RED

With your dominant hand in a 1 handshape, start at the chin and pull your index finger down a few inches, curling the finger as you do.

PINK

With your dominant hand in a K handshape, start at the chin and pull your hand down a few inches.

ORANGE

With your dominant hand in a loose fist held under your chin, squeeze the fist two times.

BLUE

With your dominant hand in a B handshape, make a repeated, outward twisting motion from the wrist.

BLACK

With your dominant hand in a 1 handshape, palm facing down, swipe your index finger across your forehead.

GREEN

With your dominant hand, form the letter G. Make a repeated, outward twisting motion from the wrist.

BROWN/TAN
With your dominant hand in a B handshape starting at the forehead, move your hand down to your chin.

PURPLE
With your dominant hand, form the letter P. Make a repeated, outward twisting motion from the wrist.

WHITE
With your dominant hand in a flat handshape against your chest, pull the hand away from your chest, and change the handshape to an O.

GRAY
Starting with both hands in 5 handshapes, move your hands back and forth, passing through the spread fingers two times.

LESSON 10.1: CHAPTER 10 VOCABULARY QUIZ

Signs Involved (in the correct order): Health, safety, colors

Instructions: This multiple-choice quiz will test your knowledge of the vocabulary you learned in this chapter. Before taking this assessment, feel free to review the vocabulary to familiarize yourself with the signs. Look closely at the pictures and possible answers, as some answers may be similar. Then check your responses against the Answer Key (page 257).

1.

a. Blood
b. Allergies
c. Cold
d. Cough

2.

a. Band-Aid
b. Cough
c. Ambulance
d. Emergency

3.

a. Temperature
b. CPR
c. Blood
d. Cold (illness)

4.

a. Dizzy
b. Doctor
c. Allergies
d. Infection

5.

a. Nurse
b. Doctor
c. Heart
d. Sneeze

6.

a. Heart
b. Hospital
c. Feet
d. Emergency

7.

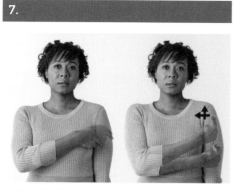

a. Hospital
b. Brain
c. Nurse
d. Feet

8.

a. Bone
b. Hurt/pain
c. Stroke
d. Nurse

9.

a. Allergy/allergies
b. Breath/breathe
c. Sick
d. Bone

10.

a. Break
b. Throw-up/vomit
c. Band-Aid
d. Grow-up

11.

a. Nurse
b. Doctor
c. Break
d. Ambulance

12.

a. Breath/breathe
b. Brain
c. Feet
d. Band-Aid

13.

a. Hair
b. Grow-up
c. Heart
d. Doctor

14.

a. Heart
b. Temperature
c. Stand
d. Skin

15.

a. Skin
b. Cold (illness)
c. Stand
d. Strong

16.

a. Red
b. Orange
c. Green
d. Pink

17.

a. Black
b. Brown
c. Blue
d. White

18.

a. Red
b. Purple
c. Brown/tan
d. Green

19.

a. White
b. Gray
c. Purple
d. Orange

20.

a. Green
b. Red
c. Brown
d. Gray

LESSON 10.2: COLOR QUESTIONS

Signs Involved (in the correct order): Colors, what, favorite

Instructions: In this two-part lesson, you'll practice asking questions using your new knowledge of color vocabulary. Part 1 focuses on asking questions; part 2 focuses on talking about your family members and their favorite colors using the listing and ordering technique we learned in chapter 7 (page 152).

Part 1: Read the following English sentences, along with their ASL translations. Practice signing each ASL translation provided. After signing each question, think about how you would respond to the question being asked. Extra challenge: For question 5, make up your own question in English, then provide and sign the ASL translation.

> **TIP:** When asking a Wh- question, keep your eyebrows down in a puzzled expression.

---

1. **English Sentence:** What is your favorite color?

ASL Translation: FAVORITE COLOR YOUR WHAT?

2. **English Sentence:** What color do you not like?

ASL Translation: COLOR YOU DON'T-LIKE WHAT?

3. **English Sentence:** What is your boyfriend's/girlfriend's favorite color?

ASL Translation: BOYFRIEND/GIRLFRIEND YOUR FAVORITE COLOR WHAT?

4. **English Sentence:** Do you have more favorite colors?

ASL Translation: FAVORITE COLORS MORE YOU HAVE?

5. **English Sentence:** _____

ASL Translation: _____

Part 2: Before continuing this lesson, review the listing and ordering technique discussed in chapter 7 (page 152). Using this technique, talk about your family members and their favorite colors. Use the following outline to write in your family members (father, mother, sister, etc.) and then write each of their favorite colors (blue, green, red, etc.). You do not have to use all the spaces provided. After you write the information, practice signing in front of a mirror or video-record yourself signing.

Use the following signing prompt to help get you started.

Signing Prompt: My mom's favorite color is blue.

ASL Translation: MOM MINE FAVORITE COLOR BLUE.

1. Family member: _____   Favorite color: _____

2. Family member: _____   Favorite color: _____

3. Family member: _____   Favorite color: _____

4. Family member: _____   Favorite color: _____

5. Family member: _____   Favorite color: _____

LESSON 10.3: MEDICAL QUESTIONS

Signs Involved: Health and safety, Wh- questions

Instructions: In this lesson, you'll practice asking and answering questions about health and medical situations.

> **TIP:** When asking a yes or no question, raise your eyebrows inquisitively.

1. **English Sentence:** English Sentence: Do you have allergies?

ASL Translation: ALLERGIES YOU HAVE?

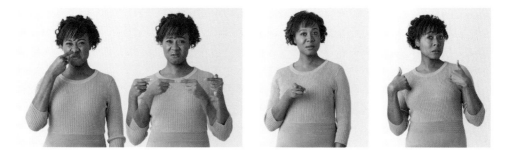

2. **English Sentence:** Where is the hospital?

ASL Translation: HOSPITAL WHERE?

3. **English Sentence:** Who is the doctor?

ASL Translation: DOCTOR WHO?

4. **English Sentence:** Are you coughing or sneezing?

ASL Translation: COUGHING SNEEZING YOU WHICH?

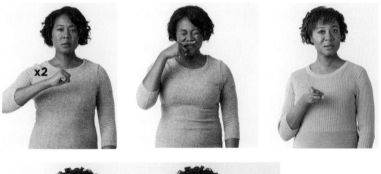

5. **English Sentence:** What's your temperature?

ASL Translation: TEMPERATURE YOURS WHAT?

6. **English Sentence:** Do you feel sick?

ASL Translation: SICK YOU FEEL YOU?

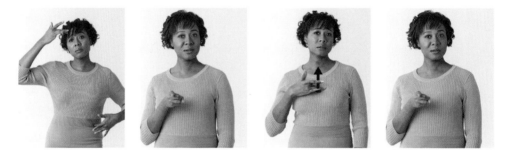

7. **English Sentence:** Which medicine do you take?

ASL Translation: MEDICINE TAKE-PILL WHAT?

8. **English Sentence:** What pain do you have?

ASL Translation: PAIN YOU HAVE WHAT?

LESSON 10.4: GET HELP

Signs Involved (in the correct order): Health and safety, Wh- questions

Instructions: In this two-part exercise, you'll practice expressing what you need and feel.

Part 1: Use the signing prompt to help you express what you need. Feel free to explore additional words from this book to express what you need.

Signing Prompt: I NEED_____.

_____.

- ▦ Doctor
- ▦ Medicine
- ▦ Hospital
- ▦ Ambulance

- ▦ Band-Aid
- ▦ Rx
- ▦ Appointment

Part 2: Use the signing prompts to help you express how you are feeling.

Signing Prompt: I HAVE _____.

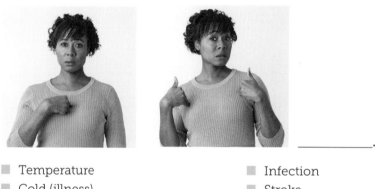

_____.

- ▦ Temperature
- ▦ Cold (illness)
- ▦ Sneezing
- ▦ Coughing

- ▦ Infection
- ▦ Stroke
- ▦ Emergency

BONUS LESSON: FINAL EXERCISE

The following phrases are a great way to expand on the vocabulary words you have learned so far. The phrases provided are part of common, everyday conversations. Although this exercise does not have an answer key, don't worry. You're on your way; just remember to use your knowledge of ASL translation to help facilitate your practice.

Can you pass the _____?

How much money do you need?

Can I please have _____?

Would you like to meet for a drink?

How far do you drive to work?

What days do you work?

ANSWER KEY

CHAPTER 3: LESSON 3.3

1. B
2. C
3. A
4. C
5. B
6. A
7. C
8. D
9. C
10. A
11. B
12. A
13. A
14. C
15. C

CHAPTER 4: LESSON 4.4

1. A
2. C
3. B
4. C
5. D
6. A
7. D
8. C
9. B
10. A
11. C
12. B
13. D
14. C
15. B
16. C
17. A
18. B
19. A
20. B

CHAPTER 5: LESSON 5.1

1. Winter
2. Fall
3. Rain
4. Summer
5. Sun
6. Weather
7. Spring
8. Snow
9. Hot

1.

2.

3.

4.

5.

CHAPTER 6: LESSON 6.1

1. Past Tense
2. Future Tense

3. Past Tense
4. Present Tense

LESSON 6.2

1. **English Sentence:** My dad cooked dinner last Thursday.
   ASL Translation: LAST THURSDAY MY DAD COOKED DINNER.

2. **English Sentence:** On Wednesday, my brother will clean the bathroom.
   ASL Translation: WEDNESDAY MY BROTHER CLEAN BATHROOM WILL.

3. **English Sentence:** When is your grandpa going to work?
   ASL Translation: GRANDPA YOURS GOING-TO WORK WHEN?

4. **English Sentence:** Dakota will celebrate his birthday next month.
   ASL Translation: NEXT MONTH D-A-K-O-T-A BIRTHDAY CELEBRATE WILL.

LESSON 6.4

1. B	6. B	11. D
2. C	7. A	12. B
3. A	8. D	13. A
4. D	9. B	14. C
5. C	10. A	15. D

CHAPTER 7: LESSON 7.1

1. A	6. D	11. B
2. C	7. B	12. C
3. B	8. C	13. D
4. D	9. D	14. C
5. A	10. A	15. B

CHAPTER 8: LESSON 8.2

1.

My brother's/sister's anniversary month is _____.

2.

My _____ does not like to celebrate _____.

3.

My _____ spent $400 to see a baseball game. It was expensive/cheap.

4.

_____ number

_____.

My parents got married when they were (age) _____.

LESSON 8.3

1. A
2. B
3. A
4. C
5. B

6. C
7. A
8. D
9. C
10. A

11. C
12. B
13. A
14. B
15. C

CHAPTER 9: LESSON 9.1

1.

2.

3.

4.

or

5.

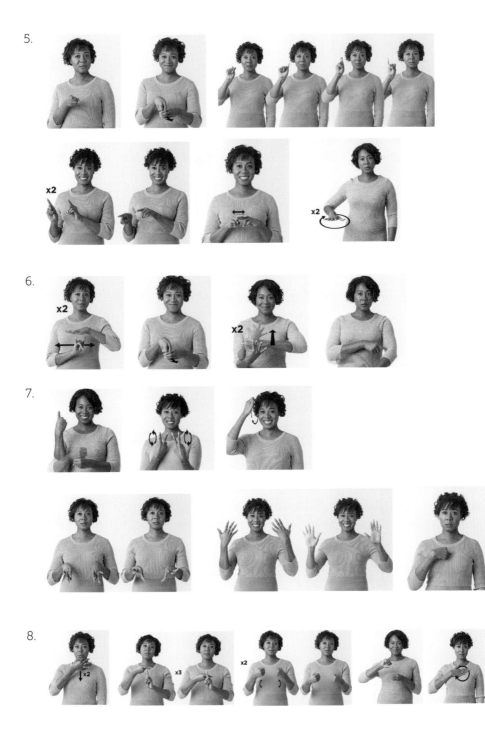

6.

7.

8.

MONDAY

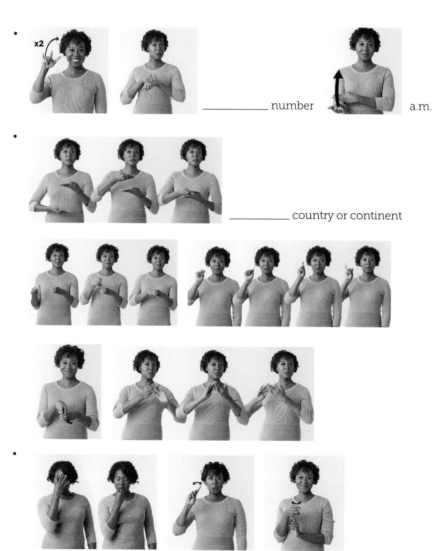

_____ number   a.m.

_____ country or continent

TUESDAY

-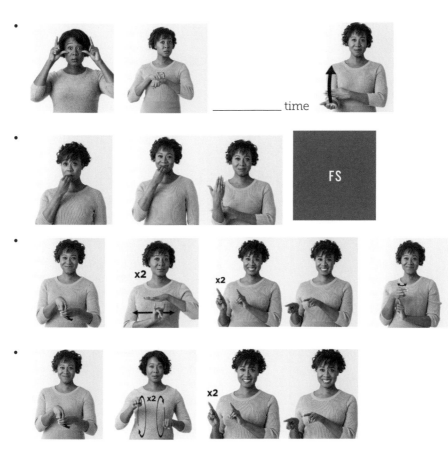

_____ time

FS

WEDNESDAY

- _____ time

-

-

-

_____ (verb)

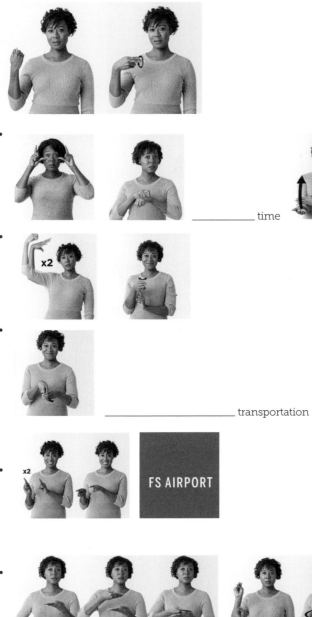

_____ time

_____ transportation

FRIDAY

-

-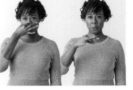

-

_____ time of day

SATURDAY

SUNDAY

-

-

-

LESSON 9.3

1. B	10. A	19. D
2. C	11. C	20. A
3. A	12. B	21. D
4. B	13. A	22. C
5. D	14. D	23. A
6. C	15. C	24. C
7. B	16. A	25. D
8. D	17. C	
9. B	18. B	

CHAPTER 10: LESSON 10.1

1. B	8. B	15. D
2. C	9. C	16. A
3. D	10. B	17. C
4. A	11. A	18. D
5. B	12. B	19. C
6. D	13. A	20. D
7. A	14. B	

RESOURCES

As you reflect on your learning from this book, I hope that you will continue to explore American Sign Language (ASL) and all the doors it opens for you and your signing community. To further your education and mastery of the language, I highly recommend signing up for courses/classes at a university or college. There are many ways to help further your receptive and expressive skills in ASL. A common one is to join a local Deaf group in your community. Search for Deaf groups on social media outlets like Facebook, MeetUp, and Instagram. You can also search online for local Deaf community groups and classes that may be available. Gatherings and classes can be found at local libraries and community centers. ASL events and conventions are held in various states for members of the Deaf community. These events and conventions will give you wonderful opportunities to practice with Deaf and hard of hearing people.

RECOMMENDED BOOKS

American Sign Language Dictionary (3rd Edition) by Martin L.A. Sternberg

The Gallaudet Dictionary of American Sign Language edited by Clayton Valli

Master ASL! Level One by Jason E. Zinza

Signing Naturally Student Workbook (Units 1–6) by Cheri Smith

WEBSITES

Gallaudet University

Gallaudet.edu

Educational resources and programs for Deaf and hard of hearing individuals.

HandSpeak

HandSpeak.com

An ASL resource containing an interactive sign language video dictionary, kids' workbook, and more.

Lifeprint

Lifeprint.com

An ASL resource containing an interactive sign language video dictionary and more, created by ASL University.

National Association of the Deaf

NAD.org

This organization's website contains a comprehensive library of learning and advocacy resources for the Deaf, hard of hearing, and their families.

Signing Savvy

SigningSavvy.com

An ASL resource containing an interactive sign language video dictionary, one-on-one tutoring, and more.

YouTube accounts to follow for video practice:

@ASLThat
@DEAFiningASL
@BillVicars

REFERENCES

HandSpeak. "Identify Different Classes of Classifiers." Accessed January 28, 2022. Handspeak.com/learn/index.php?id=20.

HandSpeak. "The History of Sign Language Linguistics." Accessed January 28, 2022. Handspeak.com/learn/index.php?id=441.

Gallaudet University. "About Thomas Hopkins Gallaudet." Accesed January 28, 2022. Gallaudet.edu/about/history-and-traditions/thomas-hopkins -gallaudet.

Jay, Michelle. "History of American Sign Language." Start ASL (blog). February 15, 2021. StartASL.com/history-of-american-sign-language.

Vicars, Bill. "ASL Classifiers." Accessed January 28, 2022. Lifeprint.com/asl101 /pages-signs/classifiers/classifiers-frame.htm.

Waterfield, Sophia. "ASL Day 2019: Everything You Need to Know about American Sign Language." *Newsweek*. April 15, 2019. Newsweek.com /asl-day-2019-american-sign-language-1394695.

INDEX

A

Afraid, 54
Africa, 193
Afternoon, 88
Age, 171
Airplane, 184
Alarm, 85
All-day, 103
All-done, 200
Allergy/allergies, 213
All-night, 103
Alphabet, 17–19
Almost, 119
Ambulance, 213
America, 194
American School for
    the Deaf, 5
American Sign
    Language (ASL)
  dialects, 6
  history of, 4–5
  as a living language, 7
  parameters for signing,
    8–10, 101
  tips and strategies for
    learning, 1–4

Angry, 54
Anniversary, 160
Appearance, 86
Apple, 130
Appointment, 214
Area, 194
Arrive, 197
Art, 158
Asia, 194
Athlete, 159
At-last, 202
Attention, getting a
    deaf person's, 47
Attractive, 86
Aunt, 38
Australia, 195

B

Back-and-forth, 184
Band-aid, 214
Bankrupt, 175
Baseball, 158
Basketball, 158
Bath, 86
Bathroom, 86

Bawl, 55
Beach, 195
Bed, 87
Beer, 130
Best-friend, 42
Bicycle, 185
Birth, 161
Birthday, 161
Black (color), 227
Black American Sign
    Language (BASL), 3
Blood, 215
Blue, 227
Boat, 185
Body language, 53
Bone, 221
Bored, 55
Boy, 35
Boyfriend, 167
Brain, 222
Brave, 56
Bread, 130
Break (fracture), 222
Break-down
    (engine), 185
Breakfast, 131
Breath/breathe, 222

Broke, 175
Brother, 38
Brown, 228
Brush-teeth, 87
Buy, 118

C

Candy, 131
Car, 186
Celebrate, 160
Cents, 173
Charge, 172
Chase, 187
Chat, 80
Cheap, 172
Child/children, 39
Chocolate, 132
Chore, 117
Christmas, 161
Church, 113
City, 114
Clean, 32
Clerc, Laurent, 5
Close-by, 186
Coffee, 132
Cold (illness), 215
Cold (temperature), 92
Color/colorful, 226
Commute, 187
Compete/
    competitor, 159
Concern, 56
Confident, 56
Confused, 56
Connecticut Asylum
    for the Education

and Instruction of
    Deaf and Dumb
    Persons, 5
Cook, 87
Cookie, 133
Corner, 196
Cost, 172
Cough, 215
Counting, 20–24
Country, 114
Cousin, 39
CPR, 216
Crackers, 133
Crazy, 57
Cry, 57
Curious, 57

D

Dad, 36
Daily, 104
Dairy, 139
Dance, 80
Daughter, 39
Day, 104
Deaf (sign), 40
Deaf community, 212
Dentist, 168
Depicting verbs, 15
Depressed, 58
Dialects, 6
Dinner, 133
Disappointed, 58
Divorced, 170
Dizzy, 216
Doctor, 216
Dollar, 173

Dominant hand
    signing, 3, 13
Don't, 55
Don't-have, 146
Don't-like, 145
Don't-understand, 69
Don't-want, 145
Double consecutive
    letters, fingerspelling,
    13, 19
Drink, 134
Drive, 186
Duty, 117

E

Earth, 196
East, 114
Easter, 162
Easy, 119
Eat, 134
Egg, 134
Embarrassed, 58
Emergency, 217
Engaged (to be
    married), 162
Enjoy, 59
Europe, 196
Evening, 93
Event, 59
Everyday, 104
Excited, 59
Exercise, 80
Exhausted, 68
Expensive, 174

F

Facial-expression (sign), 59
Facial expressions, 11, 53, 54
Fall (season), 90
Family, 41
Far, 197
Farm/farmer, 168
Fasting, 164
Father-in-law, 41
Favorite, 225
Feast, 134
Fee, 172
Feel, 60
Feelings and emotions exercises, 70–73
Feel-sorry-for, 63
Feet, 223
Fiancé/fiancée, 169
Field, 194
Finally, 202
Fine (money), 172
Fingerspelling, 11, 13
Finished, 200
Fix, 187
Fly, 184
Follow, 187
Food, 134
Football, 159
Freeze/freezer, 135
French-fries, 135
Friday, 106
Friend, 42
Friendly, 60
From, 116
Fruit, 136
Funeral, 162
Funny, 60, 81
Future, 104

G

Gallaudet, Thomas Hopkins, 4–5
Gallaudet University, 5
Game, 81
Gasoline, 188
Get-in, 188
Get-out, 189
Girl, 36
Girlfriend, 169
Glass (material), 225
Gluten-free, 136
Good-looking, 86
Goofy, 67
Grandma, 37
Grandpa, 37
Gray, 228
Great-grandma, 37
Great-grandpa, 37
Green, 227
Greetings exercise, 44–46
Ground, 194
Grow-up, 223
Grumpy, 54
Gym, 80

H

Hair, 223
Half-hour, 107
Halloween, 163
Hamburger, 136
Handshape, 8
Happen, 107
Happy, 61
Hard-of-hearing, 43
Have, 146
He, 30
Healthy, 56
Hearing, 40
Heart, 217
Hello, 28
Hike, 81
Home, 88
Honeymoon, 163
Hospital, 217
Hot (temperature), 93
Hot-dog, 137
Hotel, 197
Hour, 107
House, 88
How-long?, 200
How-many?, 144
How-much (money)?, 144
How-old?, 171
Hug, 62
Hungry, 137
Hurt, 218
Husband, 43

I

I, 28
Ice, 135
Indicating verbs, 15
Infection, 218
Insensitive, 66

Inspired, 61
Insurance, 218
It, 30

J

Just (adverb), 119

K

Ketchup, 137
Kick, 160
Kiss-fist, 62

L

Last-week, 108
Last-year, 109
Late, 118
Lazy, 61
Left (direction), 116
Lessons
 activities & events,
  176–179
 daily routines, 96–98
 food & drink, 149–154
 greetings &
  people, 44–48
 health, safety &
  colors, 232–240
 letters & numbers,
  19, 24–25
 thoughts & feelings,
  70–73
 time & place, 119–124
 travel, 203–205

Letters, 17–19
Library, 116
Like, 145
Listing technique, 152
Location, of signs, 9
Long, 200
Long-time-ago, 201
Love, 62
Love-it, 62
Lunch, 138

M

Mad, 54
Magic, 160
Make, 82
Man, 43
Married, 170
Massieu, Jean, 5
Me, 28
Mean, 65
Meat, 138
Medicine, 218
Meet-you, 33
Mercy, 63
Midnight, 118
Milk, 139
Mine, 28
Minute, 108
Mischievous, 62
Miss-you, 58
Mom, 36
Monday, 105
Money, 174
Month/monthly, 109
Moon, 92

Morning, 83
Mosque, 113
Mother-in-law, 42
Motorcycle, 189
Movement, when
 signing, 9
Movie, 82
Music, 82
Musician, 82
My, 28

N

Name, 29
Names
 fingerspelling, 19
 name signs, 20
Naughty, 62
Negative
 statements, 72–74
Nervous, 63
Next-week, 108
Next-year, 109
Nice, 32
Night, 93
Nondominant hand
 supporting, 3
Nonmanual markers
 (NMM), 10
Noon, 118
North, 115
North-America, 198
Not, 55
Not-yet, 201
Now, 110
Numbers, 20–24

Nurse, 221
Nuts, 139

O

Obligation, 117
Old, 171
Once-in-a-while, 202
Onion, 139
Orange, 227
Ordering
    technique, 152
Ours, 31
Outside, 199

P

Pain, 218
Palm orientation, 10
Pancakes, 87
Parade, 163
Parents, 170
Partner, 171
Party, 83
Passover, 164
Past, 201
Patience, 63
Pay/payment/
    payments, 175
People, 171
Pepper (spice), 140
Person, 35
Phone numbers, 25
Pidgin Signed English
    (PSE), 3, 6
Pie, 140

Pink, 226
Pity, 63
Pizza, 140
Plain verbs, 15
Play, 83
Please, 33
Popcorn, 141
Prefer, 225
Prescription (Rx), 219
Pressure, 64
Price, 172
Pronouns, 28, 30, 32
Proud, 64
Purple, 228

R

Race, 159
Rain, 89
Ramadan, 164
Ranch/rancher, 168
Recently, 119
Red, 226
Rent (verb/noun), 109
Rental, 190
Repair, 187
Reservation, 214
Responsible, 117
Restroom, 86
Ride-in/ride-on, 190
Ridiculous, 67
Right (direction), 116
Room, 89
Rude, 65
Run, 83
Rx (prescription), 219

S

Sad, 65
Salt, 141
Sandwich, 141
Saturday, 106
Sausage, 137
Scared, 54
Season, 90
See-you-later, 35
Sell, 117
Sensitive, 66
Sentence structure, 14, 101
She, 30
Shocked, 66
Shop/shopping, 118
Shower, 89
Shy, 67
Sicard, Abbé
    Roch-Ambroise
    Cucurron, 5
Sick, 219
Signing Exact English
    (SEE), 3, 6–7
Silly, 67
Sister, 38
Skill, 84
Skin, 224
Sleep/sleepy, 84
Sneeze, 219
Snow, 93
Snowmobile, 189
Sob, 55
Soccer, 160
Soda, 142
Sometimes, 202
Son, 40

Song, 82
Soon, 203
South, 115
South-America, 198
Spaghetti, 142
Spell (magic), 160
Spring (season), 90
Stand, 224
State (noun), 199
Stokoe, William, 5
Store (noun), 117
St.-Patrick's-Day, 165
Stress, 64
Strict, 67
Stroke (medical), 220
Strong, 225
Struggle, 68
Stubborn, 68
Subway, 191
Suffer, 63
Summer, 91
Sunday, 107
Sun/sunshine, 92
Supper, 133
Sweet, 142
Swim, 84

T

Take-pill, 220
Talent, 84
Talk, 80
Tan, 228
Tater-tots, 135
Tax, 172
Taxi, 191
Tea, 143

Temperature, 224
Temple, 113
Tenses, 14–15, 101–102
Thanksgiving, 165
Thank-you, 29
Theirs, 29
Themselves, 30, 32
They, 32
Thirsty, 143
Thrilled, 59
Throw-up, 221
Thursday, 106
Ticket, 192
Time, 110
"Time, Topic,
    Comment" sentence
    structure, 14
Tired, 68
Today, 110
Toilet, 86
Tomorrow, 110
Tonight, 111
Tooth/teeth, 225
"Topic, Comment"
    sentence
    structure, 14
Town, 114
Traffic, 192
Train (noun), 193
Travel, 193
Tuesday, 105
Two-of-us, 31

U

Uncle, 37
Understand, 69

United-States, 194
Universe, 199
Upset, 69
Us, 33

V

Valentine's Day, 166
Vegetable, 143
Vegetarian, 143
Verbs, 15, 79
Veterans-Day, 166
Vocabulary quizzes
  activities &
      events, 179–181
  daily routines, 94–95
  food & drink, 146–148
  greetings &
      people, 48–51
  health, safety &
      colors, 229–231
  thoughts &
      feelings, 75–77
  time & place, 124–127
  travel, 206–209
Vomit, 221

W

Walk, 85
Want, 145
Watch (movie/tv), 85
Water, 144
Weather, 91
Wedding, 167
Wednesday, 105

Week, 112

Weekend, 112

Welcome, 34

West, 115

What?, 34

What's-up?, 34

What-time?, 110

When (statement), 107

Wh-expressions, 11, 12

White, 228

Wife, 43

Will (verb), 112

Wine, 144

Winter, 91

Woman, 44

Work, 117

Workout, 80

World, 199

Worried, 69

Y

Year, 113

Yesterday, 111

You, 30

You're welcome, 29

Yourself, 31

Your/yours, 29

ACKNOWLEDGMENTS

I would like to first thank my husband, Roger, for standing by my side through all these years and encouraging me to strive for more. I want to also thank my family and friends for always believing in me and supporting me in everything I do. Lastly, I want to thank all my teachers whom I have learned from—you have pushed and challenged me, not only to be a better teacher but also to be a role model for every student I see walk into my classroom.

ABOUT THE AUTHOR

TRAVIS BELMONTES-MERRELL is an educator, father, husband, and member of the Deaf community. Travis became hard of hearing at the age of three. He grew up in a hearing family but discovered ASL at a young age, which became his passion. He began studying ASL extensively in high school.

Travis attended the University of Texas at Arlington and majored in journalism with a minor in broadcast journalism. He worked in television news for three years, but decided he wanted to change careers and move into education. In 2018, he received a master's degree in teaching American Sign Language from the University of Northern Colorado. He served as a K–12 educator and has taught at the college and university level. Travis continues teaching high school ASL and also serves as the ASL program coordinator at the University of Texas at Arlington, his alma mater.